Spreadsheet software

Wendy Yates

Published by Osborne Books Limited
Unit 1B Everoak Estate
Bromyard Road, Worcester WR2 5HP
Tel 01905 748071
Email books@osbornebooks.co.uk
Website www.osbornebooks.co.uk

Design by Laura Ingham

Printed by CPI Group (UK) Limited, Croydon, CR0 4YY, on environmentally friendly, acid-free paper from managed forests.

British Library Cataloguing in Publication Data
A catalogue record for this book is available from the British Library

ISBN 978 1909173 552

Contents

Acknowledgements

The publisher wishes to thank the following for their help with the editing, reading and production of the book: Debbie Board, Maz Loton, Cathy Turner and Jon Moore. Thanks are also due to Laura Ingham for her designs for this series.

The publisher is indebted to the Association of Accounting Technicians for its help and advice to our author and editors during the preparation of this text.

Author

Wendy Yates has a degree in Pure Mathematics and more than thirty years programming experience, ranging from sophisticated CAD through to business systems.

Wendy has developed a variety of business models, creating comprehensive Excel Macros to automate procedures. Her most recent projects have been to develop Cashflow and Bookkeeping systems in partnership with a major accountancy firm.

Wendy has wide and varied experience of teaching IT in schools, including spreadsheets and CLAIT, and she has also delivered IT courses at South Worcestershire College.

Introduction

what this book covers

This book has been written specifically to cover the 'Spreadsheet software' Unit which is mandatory for the AAT Level 2 Diploma in Accounting and Business.

The book contains clear and practical explanations of how to create and manipulate spreadsheets.

Each chapter is followed by a set of graded exercises which will enable students to develop and practise their spreadsheet skills.

To speed up the learning process in the later exercises, Osborne Books has provided a number of spreadsheet files for free download from its website www.osbornebooks.co.uk. Access to these can be gained through the 'Products and Resources' button on the menu bar and then via the *Spreadsheet Software* book page (in the AAT Accounting section).

which spreadsheet software?

The illustrations in this text are based on Excel 2010, part of the Microsoft Office suite, but it is appreciated that a variety of software will be in use at any one time. The text therefore aims to be generic wherever possible so that all users can be catered for.

Note that the downloads referred to above are provided in two versions:

- Excel 2010 files – which can be opened in other branded software as appropriate
- CSV files – which can be used to import the required raw data into most spreadsheet programs

1 Spreadsheet basics

this chapter covers...

This chapter is an introduction for those new to spreadsheets. It explains and takes you through some of the basic concepts and techniques for working with spreadsheets.

By the time you have finished this chapter and carried out the exercises which follow, you should be competent in setting up and changing a basic spreadsheet.

Note that the step-by-step instructions given in this chapter are based on the Microsoft® Excel model, but the concepts and techniques described relate to all spreadsheet packages.

The topics covered are:

■ some preliminaries

■ what is a spreadsheet

■ dealing with worksheets

■ dealing with workbooks

■ entering data into cells

■ selecting data

■ starting formulas

SOME PRELIMINARIES

numbers

Within a spreadsheet, a series of digits (0 - 9) will be treated as a NUMBER provided there are no spaces. A number can also have a decimal point (.) eg 12.99 would be twelve point nine-nine.

To ease interpretation of a number it can include commas(,) to represent thousands eg 34,567 would represent thirty four thousand, five hundred and sixty seven.

text

Any series of characters which cannot be recognised as a number is known as TEXT.

mouse click

Whenever a CLICK of the mouse is mentioned, this is referring to a click of the LEFT mouse button. Any RIGHT mouse clicks will be specifically preceded by RIGHT. DOUBLE click refers to two clicks in quick succession of the LEFT mouse key.

undo

If at any stage you wish to **Undo** the changes which you have just made, click on the **Undo** icon (left pointing curved arrow) to remove the last edit to a cell. To remove the edit before that, click the **Undo** icon again and so on.

redo

Following an **Undo** of some changes which you have just made, if you change your mind and want to reinstate those edits, click on the **Redo** icon (right pointing curved arrow) to put the last changes back. To redo the edit before that, click the **Redo** icon again and so on.

keyboard

Keys on the keyboard which you will need to be familiar with are:

RETURN (or ENTER)	ESC
TAB	CTRL (CONTROL)

So it is worth spending a minute or two identifying where these keys are located.

menus

As with all computer programs, there is a main menu bar, with tabs identifying different options available. These are usually grouped by relevance; the common tabs which we will make use of are:

■   File, Home, Insert, Page Layout, Formulas, Data, Review and View.

It is possible your menu may differ, depending on your software installation.

Often, some of the more common options can be accessed by RIGHT mouse click.

help

If you require additional information or clarification on any action, formula or general query, **Help** is available within your spreadsheet program by clicking the **Help** icon (usually a ? in a blue circle situated to the far right of the main menu bar). Alternatively, press the F1 function key.

WHAT IS A SPREADSHEET

A spreadsheet is a grid or table of rows and columns which is used to manipulate numbers and perform calculations.

rows, columns and cells

Rows are in a horizontal direction, and are identified by numbers: 1, 2, 3, and so on. This is known as the row header.

Columns are vertical, and are identified by letters: A, B, C, and so on through the alphabet. This is known as the column header.

Columns beyond Z (26) continue in the format AA, AB, AC and so on, changing to BA, BB etc. for columns 53 and onwards.

The maximum number of rows and columns allowed in a spreadsheet is determined by the software package you are using and the memory within your computer. For Excel® you can have more than one million rows and more than 16 thousand columns if your computer has the capacity.

Where a row and column cross or intersect, it is called a **cell**.

The cell is referred to by a combination of a letter (the column header) and a number (the row header) to identify its location. This is known as a **cell reference**.

Cell reference D7 would refer to the cell at the intersection of column D (the fourth column) and row 7. See the cell highlighted on the screen image on the previous page.

The lines marking the edges of the rows and columns are called **gridlines**.

Scroll bars are provided to cater for larger spreadsheets and allow scrolling both vertically and horizontally, changing the rows and columns displayed as you move up, down and across the spreadsheet.

WORKBOOKS AND WORKSHEETS

A **workbook** is the computer file created when you start a new spreadsheet.

A **workbook** contains a group of one or more **worksheets**.

Each **worksheet** is an individual **spreadsheet**.

For example, a workbook could have two worksheets, one worksheet with data, and a second worksheet containing a chart representing the data.

files and folders

Each workbook is held as one file. A file is the computer equivalent of a paper document containing the information which you have entered. Each file has a name which you specify when it is created. This should be chosen to be meaningful and help identify what the file contains, for example: Timesheet March 2014.

To organise our files in a logical way we store related files in a **folder**, which we again name when we create it to clarify the sort of files/documents the folder will contain. For example: Timesheets 2013-2014.

create a folder

Creating a folder can be achieved by using the New Folder option, and naming the folder appropriately.

DEALING WITH WORKSHEETS

When you create a new workbook it will normally contain 3 worksheets – named Sheet1, Sheet2 and Sheet3, as can be seen in the image below.

Each worksheet has a name, which is displayed as a tab at the bottom of the spreadsheet work area.

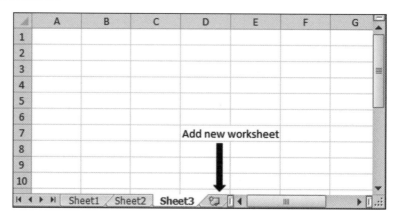

Worksheet names can be changed, by double clicking on the name tab, and entering the new name.

It is possible to add more worksheets should you require them. New worksheets are added one at a time, either by clicking on the sheet tab which has no name, but has the standard Windows symbol for a 'new' folder, or by RIGHT clicking on a worksheet name tab, selecting **Insert**, and selecting **Worksheet**.

Worksheets which are not required can be deleted, by RIGHT mouse clicking on the sheet tab to be deleted, and selecting **Delete**.

You can easily change the relative order of the worksheets within the workbook, just by selecting the name tab, holding the mouse down, and dragging the worksheet to its new position in the order.

Switching between worksheets is achieved by clicking on the name tab of the worksheet which you want to see on the screen.

Each worksheet can represent one set of data. It is also possible for data from different worksheets to be linked together to form a more complex spreadsheet. This is covered later in the book.

DEALING WITH WORKBOOKS

As described earlier, a **workbook** is a collection of worksheets ranging from one worksheet upwards to a maximum number which will be dependent on the software package and available computer memory.

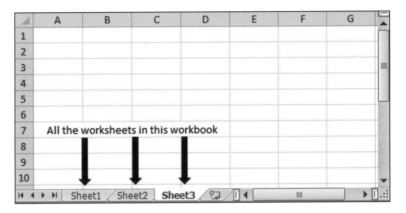

When you want to **Create** your first spreadsheet, you will select **New** from the File menu, then select **Blank Workbook** from the available templates, and a new workbook will open, usually containing three blank worksheets ready for you to enter data.

As with other computer programs, once you have entered some data into a spreadsheet, the workbook file should be regularly saved using the standard disk icon, or **Save** from the File menu.

To open a previously saved workbook, you can either select **Open** from the File menu, navigate to the required folder and select the required workbook, or if it is listed, select the workbook from the list of recently opened documents.

To save a copy of the workbook with a different name either as a backup or as a fresh starting point, you can select **Save as** from the File menu and supply a new name for the copy of the workbook.

For security purposes a copy of an important workbook should be saved to removable media such as a memory stick and stored off-site. It is also good practice to add a version number or part of a date to the filename so that different versions can be saved as the spreadsheet evolves. This also allows a previous version to be identified and opened, if required.

ENTER DATA INTO CELLS

Within the grid of cells on your worksheet, you can move around from cell to cell using various methods:

■ the mouse

■ the arrow keys

■ the **TAB** key

■ or the **RETURN** key

The current cell, known as the **active cell**, is highlighted by solid black lines, and is selected by clicking in the cell, or moving to it using one of the above methods.

The active cell reference is shown in the **Name Box** above column A; this is B5 in the example below.

To enter data into a cell:

■ click on the cell where you want the data to go

■ type your data into the cell

■ either press the **RETURN** key, or click on another cell with the mouse

Other useful keys when entering data are the **TAB** key which moves the active cell to the next cell in the current row, and the **ESC** key which cancels the current data entry.

If you just wish to edit the current data, you will see the data held in the current cell displayed in the **Formula Bar** (in this example Income forecast).

To select data:

As described above there are several ways to select an individual cell and the data it contains:

- CLICK with the mouse
- move to it with the arrow keys
- press the **TAB** key until you are on the required cell
- or press **RETURN**

Once selected, you will see the data held in the current cell displayed in the Formula Bar as described above.

If at any time you wish to select more than one cell:

- select the first cell by clicking on the cell
- keep the left mouse button pressed and drag the mouse over the other cells you wish to select

A series of selected cells is shown below.

If the cells you wish to select are not consecutive (ie next to each other)

- select the first cell by clicking on the cell
- hold down the **CONTROL** key while clicking on the other cells you want to select

An example is shown in the image below.

◢	A	B	C	D	E	F	G
1							
2							
3		February	March	April	May	June	
4							

It is often useful to be able to select multiple cells as you will see in the following chapters.

To edit or change the contents of a cell:

- select the required cell
- either enter the new data directly
- *or* click into the Formula Bar
- make any changes
- press **RETURN**

If at any time you wish to cancel the changes, press **ESC** before pressing **RETURN**, or if you have pressed **RETURN**, click on the **Undo** icon as described on page 3.

To remove data:

- select the cell to be changed
- press the **Delete** key
- *or* select **Clear Contents** from the drop down menu displayed when you right click on the cell

STARTING FORMULAS

The most powerful feature of a spreadsheet is its ability to perform calculations. To do this we use a formula. A formula identifies the cells which we use to perform the calculation on, using their cell references, and the action we want, such as addition, or subtraction.

To **create a formula**, click on the cell where you wish to place the formula. Enter the "=" sign to indicate that this cell is going to contain a formula. Once the formula has been entered the cell will display the result of the calculation from the formula.

A simple formula for **addition** might be something like =B4+B5+B6+42. This would add up the values in the cells B4, B5, B6 and the number 42, and display the result.

A simple formula for **subtraction** is: =B4–B5. The value in cell B5 is subtracted from the value in cell B4.

For **multiplication**: =B4*B5. This is the value in cell B4 multiplied by the value in cell B5. You see here that the symbol for multiply is an asterisk *.

And **division**: =B4/B5. This is the value of cell B4 divided by the value of cell B5, where the forward slash symbol / is used to denote division.

When we have a cell reference in a formula, the value within that cell is used in the calculation.

Example spreadsheet

A practical example is shown in the image below, where we want to calculate the total hours worked for each week. Columns B, C, D, E, F each represent the number of hours worked each day, for one week, Monday to Friday, represented by the rows 4 through to 8.

B10			▼	f_x	=B4+B5+B6+B7+B8		
	A	B	C	D	E	F	G
1	Hours worked						
2							
3	Week Beg	1st Apr	8th Apr	15th Apr	22nd Apr	29th Apr	
4	Mon	6	7	7	8	6.5	
5	Tue	7.5	6.5	7	7.5	7.5	
6	Wed	5	7.5	7	6	8	
7	Thu	7	6.5	6.5	7.5	7	
8	Fri	8	7.5	7.5	5	8	
9							
10	Totals	33.5					
11							

Sheet1 Sheet2 Sheet3

To calculate totals for each of the weeks, we would enter formulas in cells B10 through to F10. The formula we can enter in cell B10 to add up the hours worked in the week of 1st of April (column B), is:

=B4+B5+B6+B7+B8

As you can see this formula is displayed in the formula bar, when we have B10 selected. We would add formulas for each of the other weeks, in cells C10, D10, E10 and F10 to complete the spreadsheet.

We will create this spreadsheet in Exercise 3.

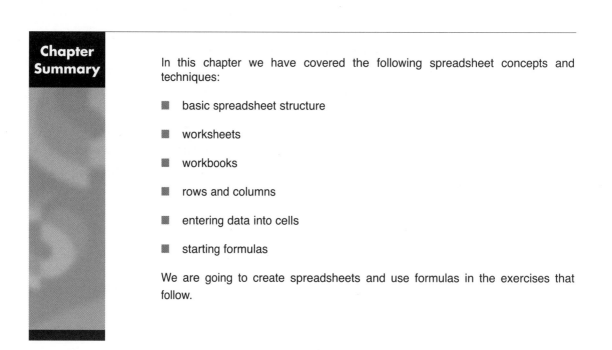

Chapter Summary

In this chapter we have covered the following spreadsheet concepts and techniques:

- basic spreadsheet structure

- worksheets

- workbooks

- rows and columns

- entering data into cells

- starting formulas

We are going to create spreadsheets and use formulas in the exercises that follow.

Activities

Exercise 1 – setting up a new worksheet and using simple formulas

In this exercise, we will create our first spreadsheet, practise moving around the spreadsheet, enter numbers, enter text, and create some simple formulas.

Stage 1

This stage is about creating a simple formula for addition:

1. Create a **New** workbook.

2. Move to Sheet1.

3. Move to cell A2, using the arrow keys, or by clicking on the cell with the mouse, enter **Add**.

4. Move to cell A3, enter **191**.

5. Move to cell A4, enter **244**.

6. In cell A6, enter the formula to **add** cells A3 and A4.

   Cell A6 should now show 435, the result of 191 + 244.

7. Save the workbook with the name **Ch1Exercise1**.

Your spreadsheet should appear as shown in the screen below:

Stage 2

This stage is about creating a simple formula for subtraction:

1. In cell C2, enter **Subtract**.

2. Move to cell C3, enter **188**.

3. Move to cell C4, enter **99**.

4. In cell C6, enter the formula to **subtract** cells C3 and C4.

   Cell C6 should now show 89, the result of 188 – 99.

5. Save the workbook.

Your spreadsheet should appear as shown in the screen below:

	A	B	C	D	E	F	G
			C6			f_x =C3-C4	
1							
2	Add		Subtract				
3	191		188				
4	244		99				
5							
6	435		89				
7							
8							
9							
10							

Sheet1 / Sheet2 / Sheet3

Stage 3

Now to create a simple formula to multiply two numbers:

1. In cell E2, enter **Multiply**.

2. Move to cell E3, enter **44**.

3. Move to cell E4, enter **2**.

4. In cell E6, enter the formula to **multiply** cells E3 and E4.

   Cell E6 should now show 88, the result of 44 x 2.

5. Save the workbook.

Your spreadsheet should appear as shown in the screen at the top of the next page:

	A	B	C	D	E	F	G
					E6 ▾	*fx*	=E3*E4

	A	B	C	D	E	F	G
1							
2	Add		Subtract		Multiply		
3	191		188		44		
4	244		99		2		
5							
6	435		89		88		
7							
8							
9							
10							

Sheet1 / Sheet2 / Sheet3

Stage 4

Finally, we are going to enter a formula to divide two numbers:

1.   In cell G2, enter **Divide**.

2.   Move to cell G3, enter **45**.

3.   Move to cell G4, enter **20**.

4.   In cell G6, enter the formula to **divide** cell G3 by G4.

     Cell G6 should now show 2.25, the result of 45 divided by 20.

5.   Save the workbook.

Your spreadsheet should appear as shown in the screen below:

					G6 ▾	*fx*	=G3/G4

	A	B	C	D	E	F	G
1							
2	Add		Subtract		Multiply		Divide
3	191		188		44		45
4	244		99		2		20
5							
6	435		89		88		2.25
7							
8							
9							
10							

Sheet1 / Sheet2 / Sheet3

Stage 5

We are now going to see that when we change a value used in a formula, the formula automatically recalculates using the new value. **This is a very important feature of spreadsheets.**

1. Change cell A3 to 192.

2. Change cell C4 to 88.

3. Change cell E3 to 40.

4. Change cell G4 to 22.5.

Your spreadsheet should now look as shown below:

	G6			f_x	=G3/G4			
	A	B	C	D	E	F	G	
1								
2	Add		Subtract		Multiply		Divide	
3	192		188		40		45	
4	244		88		2		22.5	
5								
6	436		100		80		2	
7								
8								
9								
10								

Sheet1 Sheet2 Sheet3

5. Save and **Close** the workbook.

We have now completed the first exercise.

Exercise 2 – worksheets within a workbook

In this second exercise we are going to manipulate the number of worksheets we have in our workbook, and their name tabs.

Stage 1

This first stage is to re-open the workbook Ch1Exercise1 which we have just created. We will save it with a new name to use in Exercise 2.

1. **Open** the workbook **Ch1Exercise1** created above.

2. **Save** the workbook with a new name **Ch1Exercise2** (using **Save As**).

    You will now work with this workbook **Ch1Exercise2**.

3. **Rename** Sheet1 with our data on, to **Examples** (**Double Click** on the name tab and change).

4. **Delete** Sheet2 (**Right mouse**, on the Sheet3 tab, and select **Delete**).

5. **Delete** Sheet3.

6. Save your workbook.

Your workbook should now look as follows:

	A	B	C	D	E	F	G
	G6				fx	=G3/G4	
1							
2	Add		Subtract		Multiply		Divide
3	192		188		40		45
4	244		88		2		22.5
5							
6	436		100		80		2
7							
8							
9							
10							

Examples

Stage 2

1. Add a new worksheet to the workbook (click on the **new folder** tab).

   You will see a new worksheet tab – which will automatically be selected, so you will no longer see the data on the **Examples** sheet, until you re-select the **Examples** tab.

2. Rename this new worksheet as **New Sheet** (**Double Click** on the name tab and change).

3. Select the **Examples** worksheet (**Click** on the **Examples** tab).

Your workbook should now look as follows:

	G6				f_x	=G3/G4		
	A	B	C	D	E	F	G	
1								
2	Add		Subtract		Multiply		Divide	
3	192		188		40		45	
4	244		88		2		22.5	
5								
6	436		100		80		2	
7								
8								
9								
10								

Examples / New Sheet

We are now going to change the order of the worksheets in our workbook.

4. Move **New Sheet** to before the **Examples** worksheet (**Click** on **New Sheet**, and drag to before **Examples**).

5. Save the workbook.

Your workbook should now look as follows:

	A1				f_x		
	A	B	C	D	E	F	G
1							
2							
3							
4							
5							
6							
7							
8							
9							
10							

New Sheet / Examples

Exercise 3 – setting up a structured worksheet

In this third exercise we will create the simple spreadsheet mentioned on page 11, where we record and total the hours worked for each week starting in April.

Stage 1

The first stage is to enter some text to form the basic layout of our spreadsheet:

1. Create a **New** workbook.

2. Move to Sheet1.

3. Move to cell A1, enter **Hours worked**.

4. Move to cell A3, enter **Week Beg**.

5. Enter **Mon**, **Tue**, **Wed**, **Thu**, **Fri** in cells A4, A5, A6, A7 and A8 respectively.

6. Enter **1st Apr**, **8th Apr**, **15th Apr**, **22nd Apr**, **29th Apr** in cells B3, C3, D3, E3 and F3 respectively.

7. Change the name of the sheet to **Time data**.

8. Save the workbook with the name **Ch1Exercise3**.

Your spreadsheet should appear as shown in the screen below:

Stage 2

We are going to enter some values for the hours worked:

1. For Week Beg 1st Apr, enter **6, 7.5, 5, 7, 8** in cells B4, B5, B6, B7 and B8 respectively.

2. For 8th Apr, enter 7, 6.5, 7.5, 6.5, 7.5 in cells C4, C5, C6, C7 and C8 respectively.

3. Now you have entered some data, you should save your spreadsheet (keeping the same name: **Ch1Exercise3**).

Note: It is important to save your work regularly.

Row 10 is going to contain the totals for each of the five weeks, where we have entered our hours.

4. In cell A10 enter **Totals**.

5. Now create a formula to total the hours for 1st Apr (B4, B5, B6, B7, B8) in cell B10.

6. Similarly, for the hours for 8th Apr, create a formula in C10.

7. Save your spreadsheet.

Your spreadsheet should appear as shown in the screen below:

C10		fx	=C4+C5+C6+C7+C8				
	A	B	C	D	E	F	G
1	Hours worked						
2							
3	Week Beg	1st Apr	8th Apr	15th Apr	22nd Apr	29th Apr	
4	Mon	6	7				
5	Tue	7.5	6.5				
6	Wed	5	7.5				
7	Thu	7	6.5				
8	Fri	8	7.5				
9							
10	Totals	33.5	35				

Time data / Sheet2 / Sheet3

Stage 3

We are now going to enter values for the remaining weeks.

1. In column D (15th Apr), enter 7, 7, 7, 6.5, 7.5 in cells D4, D5, D6, D7 and D8.

2. Now complete column E (22nd Apr), with values 8, 7.5, 6, 7.5, 5 in cells E4 through to E8.

3. Finally in column F (29th Apr), enter 6.5, 7.5, 8, 7, 8 in cells F4 through to F8.

All the hours worked have now been entered, we just need to complete the totals for the remaining weeks of 15th, 22nd and 29th April.

4. Create the formulas in D10, E10 and F10 to total the hours for each of the weeks.

5. Save your spreadsheet.

Your spreadsheet is now completed, and should look as shown below:

	F10			f_x	=F4+F5+F6+F7+F8		
	A	B	C	D	E	F	G
1	Hours worked						
2							
3	Week Beg	1st Apr	8th Apr	15th Apr	22nd Apr	29th Apr	
4	Mon	6	7	7	8	6.5	
5	Tue	7.5	6.5	7	7.5	7.5	
6	Wed	5	7.5	7	6	8	
7	Thu	7	6.5	6.5	7.5	7	
8	Fri	8	7.5	7.5	5	8	
9							
10	Totals	33.5	35	35	34	37	

Time data / Sheet2 / Sheet3

Stage 4

We have just realised that some of the hours are incorrect, and we need to make some changes to the numbers.

1. Week 1st Apr, is all incorrect, select cells B4 to B8.
2. Clear the existing data B4 to B8 (**Right click**, and **Clear Contents**).
3. Enter new values 7, 6.5, 5.5, 6.5, 7.5 in cells B4 to B8 respectively.
4. Change the hours for Mon in week 8th Apr to 8.5 (Cell C4).
5. Change the hours for Fri in week 29th Apr to 7.5 (Cell F8).

    You should see that all the **Totals** have recalculated.

6. Save your spreadsheet.

The new Totals should be as shown in the image below:

	B9	▾	⌐	f_x				▾
◢	A	B	C	D	E	F	G	
1	Hours worked							
2								
3	Week Beg	1st Apr	8th Apr	15th Apr	22nd Apr	29th Apr		
4	Mon	7	8.5	7	8	6.5		
5	Tue	6.5	6.5	7	7.5	7.5		
6	Wed	5.5	7.5	7	6	8		
7	Thu	6.5	6.5	6.5	7.5	7		
8	Fri	7.5	7.5	7.5	5	7.5		
9								
10	Totals	33	36.5	35	34	36.5		

| ◄ ◄ ► ►| | **Time data** | Sheet2 | Sheet3 | ⏳ | | | | |

You have now completed all the exercises for Chapter 1.

2 **Edits**

this chapter covers...

This chapter covers some more of the fundamentals, such as copy and paste, moving data around, and manipulating rows and columns.

By the time you have finished this chapter and carried out the exercises which follow, you should be comfortable with simple formulas, modifying the layout of your spreadsheet, and inserting rows and columns.

Note that the step-by-step instructions given in this chapter are based on the Microsoft® Excel model, but the concepts and techniques described relate to all spreadsheet packages.

The topics covered are:

■ *copying and moving cells*

■ *inserting and deleting rows and columns*

■ *changing the height of a row or the width of a column*

■ *more on formulas*

■ *mathematical operators*

■ *functions, an introduction*

■ *ranges*

■ *autosum*

■ *copying formulas*

COPYING AND MOVING CELLS

When we are creating a spreadsheet, we quite often want the same number, text or formula in several places, so we are able to **copy** bits of information from one or more cells and **paste** them somewhere else in the spreadsheet.

The simplest method of copying data in a cell is to:

- move to the cell you wish to copy
- from the Home menu, select **Copy**
- move to the cell where you wish to place the copy
- from the Home menu select **Paste**

If you wish to paste the data into more than one cell, select all the cells where the data is to go, then select **Paste**.

Alternatively, to copy the selected cell, you could click on the **Copy** icon on the tool bar if there is one,

or press **CTRL** and **C** together;

then to paste, click on the **Paste** icon,

or press **CTRL** and **V** together.

It is also possible to move or copy the contents of one cell to a new cell reference:

- click on the data cell to move
- from the Home menu select **Cut** or press **CTRL** and **X** together
- move to the cell where the data is to go
- from the Home menu select **Paste** or **CTRL** and **V** together

You will see the data move to the new location.

If at any time you wish to copy more than one cell at a time:

- select the cells to copy by clicking on the first cell
- keeping the left mouse button pressed drag the mouse in the appropriate direction until all the required cells are selected
- select **Copy** and **Paste** as described above

Alternatively, click on the first cell, move to the last of the cells to be selected, hold down the **SHIFT** key and click the mouse.

If the cells which you wish to copy are not consecutive, for each of the cells to be copied, hold down the **CTRL** key and click the cell.

◢	A	B	C	D	E	F	G
1							
2							
3		February	March	April	May	June	
4							

WORKING WITH ROWS AND COLUMNS

On a worksheet, each column is identified by a letter or combination of letters; this is called the **Column header**.

Similarly each row is identified by a number called the **Row header**.

◢	A	B	C	D	E	F	G
1							
2							
3				Column header			
4							
5		Row header					
6							
7							

One click on a column header will select the entire column. Similarly with a row header, one click on the row header will select the whole row.

If you realise that you have missed out a row or a column once you have entered data, it is straightforward to insert extra rows or columns.

inserting a column

■ select the column to the right of where you want to insert another column, by right clicking on the column header

■ select **Insert** from the menu displayed

The new column will be inserted at the position of the selected column, and all existing columns will move right, as shown in the example below. You can then enter data in the new column.

Note that for some spreadsheet packages you may need to select **Insert**, then **Column** from the menus.

inserting a row

■ select the row below where you want to insert another row, by right clicking on the row header

■ select **Insert** from the menu displayed; for some spreadsheet packages you may need to select **Insert**, then **Row** from the menu

In the two screens on the next page a new blank row has been inserted between the rows for Salaries and Rent (rows 5 and 6). Note that the new row will be inserted at the selected row (row 6), and all the existing rows will then move down. You can then enter data in the new row.

	A	B	C	D	E	F	G	
1	Expenditure forecast							
2								
3		January	February	March	April	May	June	
4								
5	Salaries							
6	Rent							
7	Accountancy							
8	Advertising							
9	Postage							
10	Stationery							
11								

	A	B	C	D	E	F	G	
1	Expenditure forecast							
2								
3		January	February	March	April	May	June	
4								
5	Salaries							
6								
7	Rent							
8	Accountancy							
9	Advertising							
10	Postage							
11	Stationery							

For some spreadsheet packages you may need to select **Insert**, then **Row** from the menus.

deleting a column

To delete a column:

■ select the column to be deleted, by right clicking on the column header

■ select **Delete** from the menu displayed

For some spreadsheet packages you may need to select **Delete**, then **Column** from the menus.

deleting a row

To delete a row:

■ select the row to be deleted, by right clicking on the row header

■ select **Delete** from the menu displayed

For some spreadsheet packages you may need to select **Delete**, then **Row** from the menus.

changing the width of a column

◢	A	B	C	D	E	F	G
1	Expenditure forecast						
2							
3		January	February	March	April	May	June
4							
5	Salaries						
6	Insurance						
7	Rent						
8	Accountancy						
9	Advertising						
10	Postage						

If you look at the example above, you will see that some of the text in the selected cell in column A overflows into column B. Once we put data into column B, the full text in column A will no longer be visible, so we need to make column A wider.

To make a column wider:

■ click on the column header

■ move the cursor to the line at the right edge of the column header box, the cursor changes shape to a black cross with arrow heads

■ press the mouse down

■ drag to the right as far as is required to display all information correctly

■ release the mouse

Column A is then made wider, as shown below:

◢	A	B	C	D	E	F	G
1	Expenditure forecast						
2							
3		January	February	March	April	May	June
4							
5	Salaries						
6	Insurance						
7	Rent						
8	Accountancy						
9	Advertising						
10	Postage						
11	Stationery						
12							

There are several alternative ways to make a column wider. If you double click on the boundary on the right edge of the column header box, the column will automatically widen to contain the longest data within the column.

Also if you right click on the column header, you can select Column Width from the drop down menu and specify a width as a number from 0 to 255 which represents the number of characters that can be displayed in a cell that is formatted with the standard font.

changing the height of a row

The method used to modify the height of a row is very similar:

■ click on the row header

■ move the cursor to the bottom edge of the row header box, the cursor changes shape to a black cross with arrow heads

■ press the mouse down

■ drag down or up until you are satisfied with the row height

■ release the mouse

You can see in the image below how we have made the height of row 1 containing 'Expenditure forecast' larger to make it stand out as a heading.

Also, if you right click on the row header, you can select Row Height and specify the height as a number from 0 to 409, which represents the height measurement in points (1 point equals approximately 1/72 inch or 0.35mm).

If the row height is set to zero, the row is hidden.

MORE ON FORMULAS

As we have seen in the previous chapter, whenever we wish to carry out a calculation or enter a formula into a cell within our spreadsheet, we move to the cell where we want the formula to appear and start by entering an equals sign =.

The formula can take a very simple form, containing just numbers, or a mixture of numbers and cell references.

Examples of formulas include:

=3 + 2

=D6 – 1.15

=D6 * D7

=D32

Note that as we create the formula, any spaces we insert within the formula are automatically ignored.

One of the most significant points about formulas is that when we copy a formula from one cell to another cell or group of cells, the row and column numbers automatically change as appropriate. They will automatically relate to the row or column references of the new cell to which the formula has been copied.

mathematical operators

The common mathematical operators which we will use in our formulas are as follows:

- Addition: +

- Subtraction: –

- Multiplication: *

- Division: /

We also make use of brackets: ( )

As with our normal mathematics there is an **order** that will be followed when a formula is interpreted, known as the **operator precedence**.

The order of calculations within any formula is as follows:

- any calculation contained in brackets is done first

- division and multiplication are ranked the same

- addition and subtraction are ranked the same

So, if we want to group parts of our calculation to ensure that certain parts are calculated before a subsequent part, then we would use brackets.

For example:

= (B3 + 5)/100

Here 5 is added to B3 and the result is divided by 100.

This gives a different result to

= B3+5/100

Here 5 is divided by 100 and the result is added to B3

As you can see brackets play a very important part in our construction of formulas.

FUNCTIONS – AN INTRODUCTION

Spreadsheet packages contain built-in formulas called **Functions** that make it easy to perform common calculations on data. For example, **=SUM( )** is a function which can be used to add up values.

Most functions are designed to accept values (commonly known as data) which are then used in the calculations. This data is entered within the round brackets which follow the function's name.

For example, **=SUM(A1,A2,A3)** is a formula which uses the **SUM** function to add up the values of the three cells A1, A2 and A3.

These values are also known as '**arguments**'.

As you can see, each argument (or value) is usually separated from the previous argument (value) by a comma.

The **type** of argument will vary from function to function: it could be a number, or a cell reference, or group of cells.

The **number** of arguments may also vary from function to function.

The most common forms of argument are a cell reference, or group of cell references, as we shall see in the examples which follow. Look at cell B12 in the screen at the top of the next page.

As you can see in this screen, the **SUM** function is prompting you to enter the first argument or number to be added. This could be a cell reference or an actual number.

If an argument is **optional** (i.e. you don't have to enter it) you will see the argument in square brackets, for example [number2], as shown in the image on the next page. The result which a function creates is said to be the value **returned** by the function, and is known as the **return value**.

| SUM | ▾ | × ✔ *fx* | =sum(|

◢	A	B	C	D	E	F	G	
1	Expenditure forecast							
2								
3		January	February	March	April	May	June	
4								
5	Salaries	80000						
6	Insurance	1000						
7	Rent	3500						
8	Accountancy	270						
9	Advertising	0						
10	Postage	95						
11	Stationery	57						
12	Totals	=sum(						

| ◄ ◄ ► ►| | Sheet1 | SUM(**number1**, [number2], ...) | |

ranges

A range is a **group or block of cells in a worksheet**. It is essentially a shorthand way of specifying the first and last cell and automatically including all the cells in between.

A range is identified by the cell reference of the first cell (upper left cell), followed by a colon, then the cell reference of the last cell (bottom right).

Examples of a range of cells include:

D4:D11 – all the cells are in the same column

C4:F4 – all the cells are in the same row

D4:F10 – a block of cells across several rows and columns

A range of cells as described above can be used as an argument within a function, for example **=SUM(D4:D11)**.

So if we go back to the example shown previously to total the expenditure for January, we would enter the formula **=SUM(B5:B11)** in cell B12, as shown in the image on the next page.

AUTOSUM

This is a facility available in Microsoft Excel, which may not be available in other spreadsheet packages. It provides a quick way of selecting ranges of cells, usually for totalling, without having to manually specify or select the start and end cells for the range.

You select the cell where you want to position a total, and **AUTOSUM** (represented by the greek symbol Σ) will guess which cells above, or to the left you want to add up.

In the example on the previous page, we have selected cell B12, then selected **AUTOSUM** from the menu bar. You can see that the formula **=SUM(B5:B11)** is automatically shown in the cell. If you just press **RETURN** this formula will be entered into the cell.

how to use AUTOSUM

- select a cell below the column of numbers or to the right of the row of numbers

- select **AUTOSUM** from the menu bar; a dotted rectangle will be displayed, highlighting the numbers to be included

- if the appropriate cells are included, press **RETURN**

- if not, use the mouse to drag the boundaries of the rectangle to include the appropriate cells

COPYING FORMULAS

Now we have learnt how to create formulas, it becomes clear very quickly that we can save a lot of time if once we have created a formula, we can copy it to act on other rows and columns.

As mentioned previously, when we copy a formula from one cell to another cell or group of cells, the row and column numbers automatically change as appropriate. They will automatically relate to the row or column references of the new cell to which the formula has been copied.

Copying formulas is just the same as copying other cells (text and numbers):

- move to the formula you wish to copy

- from the Home menu, select **Copy**

- move to the cell where you wish to place the copy

- from the Home menu select **Paste**

If you wish to paste the formula into more than one cell, select all the cells where the formula is to go, then select Paste.

Alternatively, to copy the selected formula, you could click on the **Copy** icon on the tool bar if there is one,

or press **CTRL** and **C** together;

then to paste, click on the **Paste** icon,

or press **CTRL** and **V** together.

Chapter Summary

In this chapter we have covered the following spreadsheet concepts and techniques:

- copying cells

- inserting and deleting rows and columns

- changing the height of a row or the width of a column

- more on formulas

- functions, an introduction

- autosum

- copying formulas

We are going to practise these techniques in the following exercises.

Activities

Exercise 1 – creating another workbook, using formulas to check data

In this exercise we will create a simple spreadsheet for bank transactions.

Stage 1

This stage involves entering some text to form the basic layout of our spreadsheet.

1. Open a new workbook.

2. Move to Sheet2.

3. Change the name of the sheet to **July**.

4. Move to cell A1, enter **Bank transactions**.

5. Move to cell A3, enter **Opening balance**.

6. Widen column A so that all text is contained within the column.

7. Enter **1500** in cell B3.

8. Enter **Date** in cell A5, **Debit** in B5, **Credit** in C5, **Balance** in D5.

9. Save the workbook with the name **Ch2Exercise1**.

Your spreadsheet should look as shown below:

	A	B	C	D	E	F
1	Bank transactions					
2						
3	Opening balance	1500				
4						
5	Date	Debit	Credit	Balance		
6						
7						
8						
9						
10						

A5 — *fx* Date

Sheet1 **July** Sheet3

Stage 2

We are going to enter details of some transactions.

1. Starting in row 6, enter **02/07/14** in column A, **95.34** in column B, **0** in column C.

2. In row 7, enter **11/07/14**, **0**, **25.5** in columns A, B, C respectively.

3. In row 8, enter **15/07/14**, **0**, **34.78** in columns A, B, C respectively.

4. In row 9, enter **22/07/14**, **67.99**, **0** in columns A, B, C respectively.

5. In row 10, enter **28/07/14**, **17.99**, **0** in columns A, B, C respectively.

6. Save your spreadsheet.

Your spreadsheet should now look as shown below:

	A	B	C	D	E	F
	C10		f_x	0		
1	Bank transactions					
2						
3	Opening balance	1500				
4						
5	Date	Debit	Credit	Balance		
6	02/07/2014	95.34	0			
7	11/07/2014	0	25.5			
8	15/07/2014	0	34.78			
9	22/07/2014	67.99	0			
10	28/07/2014	17.99	0			
11						

Sheet1 **July** Sheet3

Stage 3

We are now going to enter some formulas to calculate the balance after each transaction.

1. On the first row of data (row 6) the value in the Balance column is going to be calculated using the opening balance. Enter a formula in cell D6, which takes the opening balance (B3), subtracts the debit (B6), and adds the credit (C6).

2. Enter the formula in D7, which uses the previous balance from D6, subtracts the debit (B7), and adds the credit (C7).

3. Enter a formula for the remaining rows of data.

4. Save your spreadsheet.

Your spreadsheet should now look as shown on the next page:

D6	▼ (	f_x	=B3-B6+C6			▼
	A	B	C	D	E	F
1	Bank transactions					
2						
3	Opening balance	1500				
4						
5	Date	Debit	Credit	Balance		
6	02/07/2014	95.34	0	1404.66		
7	11/07/2014	0	25.5	1430.16		
8	15/07/2014	0	34.78	1464.94		
9	22/07/2014	67.99	0	1396.95		
10	28/07/2014	17.99	0	1378.96		
11						

Sheet1 | **July** | Sheet3

Stage 4

We are now going to finalise the spreadsheet and enter some formulas to carry out some cross checks.

1. Enter **Closing balance** in cell A4.

2. Insert a row between row 4 and row 5.

3. The value of the closing balance will be the balance after the last transaction (D11 in this instance).

    Enter a formula in B4 so that this cell always holds the value of D11.

4. The transaction of 28/07/14 is incorrect, the Debit figure should be 107.99. Change the value in cell B11; see how the value in B4 changes to the new closing balance figure.

5. Enter **Totals** in cell A12.

6. Enter a formula in cell B12 to total the debits. (Adding up B7 through to B11.)

7. Enter a formula in cell C12 to total the credits.

8. In cell E12, enter a formula which takes the opening balance, subtracts the total debits, and adds in the total credits. (This should give the same value as the closing balance – a useful reconciliation.)

9. Save your spreadsheet.

Your spreadsheet should now appear as shown at the top of the next page:

	A	B	C	D	E	F
	E12	▾	f_x =B3-B12+C12			
1	Bank transactions					
2						
3	Opening balance	1500				
4	Closing balance	1288.96				
5						
6	Date	Debit	Credit	Balance		
7	02/07/2014	95.34	0	1404.66		
8	11/07/2014	0	25.5	1430.16		
9	15/07/2014	0	34.78	1464.94		
10	22/07/2014	67.99	0	1396.95		
11	28/07/2014	107.99	0	1288.96		
12	Totals	271.32	60.28		1288.96	
13						

Sheet1   **July**   Sheet3

In our next example, we are going to look at calculating costs for manufacturing a differing number of units of a product.

Exercise 2 – setting up a costing worksheet

In this exercise, we will create a spreadsheet, insert rows and columns, create some simple formulas, and use copy and paste. The spreadsheet will be an example of production costing.

Stage 1

This stage is about creating our basic layout.

1.   Create a **New** workbook.
2.   Move to Sheet1.
3.   Enter the spreadsheet title **Production costs**.
4.   In cell B2, enter **No of units**.
5.   In C2, enter **Unit Cost**.
6.   In D2, enter **Total Cost**.
7.   In A3, enter **Materials**.
8.   In A4, enter **Labour**.
9.   Save the workbook with the name **Ch2Exercise2**.

Your workbook should look as shown below:

	A	B	C	D	E	F	
1	Production costs						
2		No of Units	Unit Cost	Total Cost			
3	Materials						
4	Labour						
5							

Stage 2

In this stage we are going to enter some values, and modify the layout.

1.   Continuing with the **Ch2Exercise2** workbook.
2.   Insert a row between the Production costs title (row1) and the column headings (row 2).
3.   Increase the height of row 1 to 25, to make it stand out more.
4.   In cell B4 enter **12000** for the No of units.
5.   Copy the value in B4 to B5.
6.   Enter the unit cost for materials (C4) **£5**.
7.   Enter the unit cost for labour (C5) **£2**.
8.   In cell D4, enter the formula to calculate the total materials cost for these 12000 units (=B4*C4).
9.   Similarly in cell D5, enter the formula for total labour costs (enter the formula directly, or copy the formula from cell D4).
10. Save the workbook.

Your workbook should look as shown below:

	D4			f_x	=B4*C4			
	A	B	C	D	E	F	
1	Production costs						
2							
3		No of Units	Unit Cost	Total Cost			
4	Materials	12000	£5	£60,000			
5	Labour	12000	£2	£24,000			
6							
7							
8							
9							

Sheet1 / Sheet2 / Sheet3

Stage 3

We are going to introduce some further values and do some more calculations.

1.   Continuing with the **Ch2Exercise2** workbook.

2.   In cell A6, enter the **Fixed Costs**.

3.   In cell D6, enter **£36000**.

4.   In cell A7, enter **Total**.

5.   In cell D7, enter the formula to calculate the sum of the Total Cost values.

It should now look as shown below:

	D7			f_x	=SUM(D4:D6)			
	A	B	C	D	E	F	
1	Production costs						
2							
3		No of Units	Unit Cost	Total Cost			
4	Materials	12000	£5	£60,000			
5	Labour	12000	£2	£24,000			
6	Fixed Costs			£36,000			
7	Total			£120,000			
8							

We will now work out the unit cost for the Fixed Costs.

6. In cell B6, enter **12000** for the no of units.

7. Enter a formula in cell C6, to calculate the unit cost for Fixed Costs (=D6/B6).

C6			f_x	=D6/B6		
	A	B	C	D	E	F
1	Production costs					
2						
3		No of Units	Unit Cost	Total Cost		
4	Materials	12000	£5	£60,000		
5	Labour	12000	£2	£24,000		
6	Fixed Costs	12000	£3	£36,000		
7	Total			£120,000		

Now we have the overall total cost for the manufacture of 12000 units we can calculate the overall unit cost based on materials, labour, and Fixed Costs.

8. Enter a formula in C7 to sum the unit costs.

9. Save the workbook.

Your workbook should look as shown below:

C7			f_x	=SUM(C4:C6)		
	A	B	C	D	E	F
1	Production costs					
2						
3		No of Units	Unit Cost	Total Cost		
4	Materials	12000	£5	£60,000		
5	Labour	12000	£2	£24,000		
6	Fixed Costs	12000	£3	£36,000		
7	Total		£10	£120,000		
8						

Exercise 3 – improving our costing worksheet

In this exercise, we take our production costing worksheet created in the previous exercise and improve the structure.

Stage 1

Changing our layout.

1. Open the workbook created in the previous exercise **Ch2Exercise2**.

2. Insert 2 rows between the current row 2, and row 3. (This should move the current row 3 down to be row 5.)

3. Copy cell B5 (No of Units) into cell A3.

4. In Cell C3 enter 12000 (or copy B6).

5. Save the workbook with name **Ch2Exercise3**.

	C3			f_x	12000			
	A	**B**	**C**	**D**	**E**	**F**		
1	Production costs							
2								
3	No of Units		12000					
4								
5		No of Units	Unit Cost	Total Cost				
6	Materials	12000	£5	£60,000				
7	Labour	12000	£2	£24,000				
8	Fixed Costs	12000	£3	£36,000				
9	Total		£10	£120,000				

What we need to do now is modify our formulas so that they all refer to the one cell which defines the number of units we want to produce (which is going to be cell C3), rather than having that value multiple times within our spreadsheet.

Stage 2

Modifying our formulas.

1. Continue with the workbook **Ch2Exercise3**.

2. Modify the formula for Total Cost for Materials (D6) to use Materials Unit Cost (C6) and No of Units (C3).

3. Similarly modify the formula for Total Cost for Labour (D7).

4. For Fixed Costs, modify the formula which calculates the Unit Cost (C8) to use Total Fixed Costs (D8) and No of Units (C3).

The values shown in the cells should look exactly as before, as shown in the image below:

	D6		▼		f_x	=C3*C6				∨
◢	A	B		C		D	E	F		▬
1	Production costs									
2										
3	No of Units			12000						
4										
5		No of Units		Unit Cost		Total Cost				
6	Materials	12000		£5		£60,000				
7	Labour	12000		£2		£24,000				
8	Fixed Costs	12000		£3		£36,000				
9	Total			£10		£120,000				

It is only the formulas which are different, as shown in the image below:

	A1	▼		f_x	Production costs		∨
◢	A		B		C	D	▬
1	Production costs						
2							
3	No of Units				12000		
4							
5			No of Units		Unit Cost	Total Cost	
6	Materials		12000		5	=C3*C6	
7	Labour		12000		2	=C3*C7	
8	Fixed Costs		12000		=D8/C3	36000	
9	Total				=SUM(C6:C8)	=SUM(D6:D8)	

The final stage is to remove column B, holding the repeated No of Units.

5.   Delete column B.

If, when you do this you get #REF appearing in any of the cells, it means you have not changed all the formulas correctly, and they are still using the values in Column B. (Use Undo to put the column back, and check each of the formulas.)

Your spreadsheet should look as follows:

B3			f_x	12000			
	A	B	C	D	E	F	G
1	Production costs						
2							
3	No of Units	12000					
4							
5		Unit Cost	Total Cost				
6	Materials	£5	£60,000				
7	Labour	£2	£24,000				
8	Fixed Costs	£3	£36,000				
9	Total	£10	£120,000				

6.   Change the No of Units to 18000.

See how making one change now reflects through all of our calculations.

A1			f_x	Production costs			
	A	B	C	D	E	F	G
1	Production costs						
2							
3	No of Units	18000					
4							
5		Unit Cost	Total Cost				
6	Materials	£5	£90,000				
7	Labour	£2	£36,000				
8	Fixed Costs	£2	£36,000				
9	Total	£9	£162,000				

If we wanted to compare the effect of two different quantities at once we could do this, by copying all the relevant cells to a new area, and the formulas will be copied.

7. Select cells B3 to C9.

8. Select **COPY**.

9. Move to cell E3, select **PASTE**.

10. Change cell B3 back to 12000.

11. Save the workbook.

You can now compare the different costings for two different levels of production, as shown in the image below.

B3				f_x	12000		
	A	B	C	D	E	F	G
1	Production costs						
2							
3	No of Units	12000			18000		
4							
5		Unit Cost	Total Cost		Unit Cost	Total Cost	
6	Materials	£5	£60,000		£5	£90,000	
7	Labour	£2	£24,000		£2	£36,000	
8	Fixed Costs	£3	£36,000		£2	£36,000	
9	Total	£10	£120,000		£9	£162,000	

You have now completed all the exercises for Chapter 2.

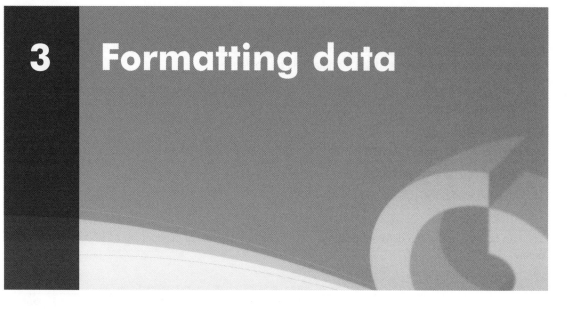

3 Formatting data

this chapter covers...

In this chapter we describe ways of formatting data within a spreadsheet using different text styles and fonts. We also explain different ways of representing numeric data, including currencies and dates.

When you have finished this chapter and carried out the exercises which follow, you should be competent in formatting a spreadsheet.

The concepts and techniques covered are:

■ *formatting – style*

■ *formatting – font*

■ *number formats*

■ *date formats*

Note that the step-by-step instructions given in this chapter are based on the Microsoft® Excel model, but the concepts and techniques described relate to all spreadsheet packages.

FORMATTING TEXT – STYLE

Text formatting within a spreadsheet, as with other types of document, is often used to make an item stand out or to emphasise specific data.

We will use the expenditure worksheet shown below as an example.

	A1	▼		*fx*	Expenditure forecast			▼
⬜	A	B	C	D	E	F	G	
1	Expenditure forecast							
2								
3		January	February	March	April	May	June	
4								
5	Salaries							
6	Insurance							
7	Rent							
8	Accountancy							
9	Advertising							
10	Postage							
11	Stationery							

◄ ◄ ► ►◄ Sheet1 / Sheet2 / **Sheet3**

making data bold

To make data bold in one cell:

■ click on the required cell

then

■ click on the **Bold** icon on the menu bar if visible

or

■ right click on the selected cell

■ select **Format cells**

■ select **Font**

■ make the font style **Bold**

or

■ press **CTRL** and **B** together (hold down the **CONTROL** key and tap the **B** key and release)

Now look at the next page to see the result.

	A	B	C	D	E	F	G
1	Expenditure forecast		◄━━━━━		Now bold		
2							
3		January	February	March	April	May	June
4							
5	Salaries						

To make data in **more than one cell bold**:

■ select all the required cells

■ follow the steps set out on the previous page

using italics

To use **italics in one cell**:

■ click on the required cell

then

■ click on the **Italics** icon on the menu bar if visible

or

■ right click on the selected cell

■ select **Format cells**

■ select **Font**

■ make the font style **Italics**

or

■ press **CTRL** and **I** together (hold down the **CONTROL** key and tap the **I** key and release)

To make **more than one cell italicised**:

■ select all the required cells

■ follow one of the formatting choices explained above

See the spreadsheet screen below:

5	*Salaries*				
6	*Insurance*				
7	*Rent*				
8	*Accountancy*	◄━━━━━ *Now Italics*			
9	*Advertising*				
10	*Postage*				
11	*Stationery*				

Sheet1 / Sheet2 / **Sheet3**

underlining data

To **underline data**:

■ click on the required cell

then

■ click on the **Underline** icon on the menu bar if visible

or

■ right click on the selected cell, select **Format cells**, select **Font** and make the underline style **Single**

or

■ press **CTRL** and **U** together (hold down the **CONTROL** key and tap the **U** key and release)

To underline data in more than one cell, select all the required cells and follow the steps set out above.

	A	B	C	D	E	F	G	
	F8			*fx*				
1	**Expenditure forecast**				Now Underlined			
2								
3		January	February	March	April	May	June	
4								
5	*Salaries*							
6	*Insurance*							
7	*Rent*							
8	*Accountancy*							
9	*Advertising*							
10	*Postage*							
11	*Stationery*							

Sheet1 / Sheet2 / **Sheet3**

To **double underline data**:

■ click on the required cell

then

■ click on the drop-down arrow by the **Underline** icon

■ select **Double** underline

or

■ right click on the selected cell, select **Format cells**, select **Font** and make the underline style **double**

An example is shown below:

	A	B	C	D	E	F	G
1	**Expenditure forecast**				Now Double Underlined		
2							
3		January	February	March	April	May	June
4							
5	*Salaries*						
6	*Insurance*						
7	*Rent*						
8	*Accountancy*						
9	*Advertising*						
10	*Postage*						
11	*Stationery*						

changing back to normal text

To turn off the style, such as bold, underline, italics, you follow exactly the same steps described above and the style will change back to normal.

FORMATTING TEXT – FONT

font face

The font face (often known as the 'font') of text is the style of the lettering:

This is Times   This is Calibri

To change the font face:

■ click on the required cell

then

■ click on the **Font face list** drop-down on the menu bar if visible

■ select the required font face

or

■ right click on the selected cell

■ select **Format cells**

■ select **Font**

■ choose the required **Font face** from the list

To change the font face in more than one cell, select all the required cells and follow the steps above.

font size

To change the font size:

■ click on the required cell

then

■ click on the **Font size** drop-down on the menu bar if visible

■ select the required font size

or

■ right click on the selected cell, select **Format cells**, select **Font** and choose the required font size from the list

To change the font size in more than one cell, select all the required cells and follow the steps above.

font colour

To change the font colour:

- click on the required cell

then

- click on the **Font colour** drop-down on the menu bar if visible (usually displayed as a capital A, with the current colour displayed as a bar underneath)
- select the required font colour

or

- right click on the selected cell, select **Format cells**, select **Font** and choose the required **Colour** from the list

To change the font colour in more than one cell, select all the required cells and follow the steps above.

NUMBER FORMATS

The word '**format**' is used in this context to describe the way in which a number will be displayed.

dealing with decimal places

When you enter a number into a cell it is displayed exactly as you type it, except that any **trailing zeros** (zeros after the last non-zero digit on the right of the decimal point), and **leading zeros** (zeros before the first non-zero digit at the front of the number) will be ignored.

For example, if you type 0000125.76000 into a cell and press **RETURN** (Enter) you will see 125.76 displayed.

If you want to see trailing zeros after a decimal point, you will need to change the number of decimal places which are displayed.

For example, if you are dealing with money amounts, you will want to see £34.10 rather than £34.1, which looks very odd. It is quite common that you would want all values in a particular column or row to display to a certain number of decimal places, so that the data in the spreadsheet looks consistent.

You can see in the example on the next page that several of the data entries are displayed with only one digit after the decimal point.

*(**Note** that throughout this example a 'credit' means a payment **into** the bank and a 'debit' means a payment **out** – just as you would see on a bank statement, but not in double-entry.)*

◢	A	B	C	D	E	F	G
1	Bank transactions						
2							
3	Opening balance	1500					
4	Closing balance	1289.05					
5							
6	Date	Debit	Credit	Balance			
7	02/07/2014	95.34	0	1404.66			
8	11/07/2014	0	25.5	~~1430.16~~	One decimal place		
9	15/07/2014	0	34.78	1464.94			
10	22/07/2014	67.9	0	1397.04			
11	28/07/2014	107.99	0	1289.05			

To change the number of decimal places:

- select the required cells, row or column

- right click on the selection

- select **Format cells**

- select the **Number** tab

- select category **Number**

- adjust the number of decimal places as required

You can see the effect below where the number formats for columns B and C have been changed to display two decimal places.

◢	A	B	C	D	E	F	G
1	Bank transactions						
2							
3	Opening balance	1500.00					
4	Closing balance	1289.05					
5							
6	Date	Debit	Credit	Balance			
7	02/07/2014	95.34	0.00	1404.66			
8	11/07/2014	0.00	25.50	1430.16			
9	15/07/2014	0.00	34.78	1464.94			
10	22/07/2014	67.90	0.00	1397.04			
11	28/07/2014	107.99	0.00	1289.05			
12	Totals	271.23	60.28		1289.05		

displaying commas in figures

In order to make numbers more readable, we often insert a comma to identify when the number is over a thousand, and a further comma for over a million and so on.

To display a , (comma) to represent thousands:

- select the required cells, row or column

- right click on the selection

- select **Format cells**

- select the **Number** tab

- select category **Number**

- tick the **Use 1000 separator** box

As you can see in the image below, the comma can make a big difference to the readability of the spreadsheet. Compare Column D below with Column D on the screen shown on the previous page.

	A	B	C	D	E	F	G
1	Bank transactions						
2							
3	Opening balance	1500.00					
4	Closing balance	1289.05					
5							
6	Date	Debit	Credit	Balance			
7	02/07/2014	95.34	0.00	1,404.66			
8	11/07/2014	0.00	25.50	1,430.16			
9	15/07/2014	0.00	34.78	1,464.94			
10	22/07/2014	67.90	0.00	1,397.04			
11	28/07/2014	107.99	0.00	1,289.05			
12	Totals	271.23	60.28		1,289.05		

dealing with currencies

Often when we are dealing with money it is simpler to use the built in **format** of **currency** for our data. A format of currency does not affect the values but merely the way the data is displayed.

One of the most commonly used currencies is the UK pound sterling.

To display data as **sterling** with a £ symbol:

- select the required cells, row or column

- right click on the selection

- select **Format cells**

- select the **Number** tab

- select category **Currency**

- adjust the decimal places as required

■ for **Symbol** select the £ (pound sterling) from the list displayed

The effect of formatting columns B, C, D and E as currency sterling is shown below:

	A	B	C	D	E	F	G
1	Bank transactions						
2							
3	Opening balance	£1,500.00					
4	Closing balance	£1,289.05					
5							
6	Date	Debit	Credit	Balance			
7	02/07/2014	£95.34	£0.00	£1,404.66			
8	11/07/2014	£0.00	£25.50	£1,430.16			
9	15/07/2014	£0.00	£34.78	£1,464.94			
10	22/07/2014	£67.90	£0.00	£1,397.04			
11	28/07/2014	£107.99	£0.00	£1,289.05			
12	Totals	£271.23	£60.28		£1,289.05		

If the values we had entered were euros, we could use the same procedure as for the pound sterling (see opposite) and select the euro as the symbol from the list displayed. The spreadsheet would then appear as follows:

	A	B	C	D	E	F	G
1	Bank transactions						
2							
3	Opening balance	€ 1,500.00					
4	Closing balance	€ 1,289.05					
5							
6	Date	Debit	Credit	Balance			
7	02/07/2014	€ 95.34	€ 0.00	€ 1,404.66			
8	11/07/2014	€ 0.00	€ 25.50	€ 1,430.16			
9	15/07/2014	€ 0.00	€ 34.78	€ 1,464.94			
10	22/07/2014	€ 67.90	€ 0.00	€ 1,397.04			
11	28/07/2014	€ 107.99	€ 0.00	€ 1,289.05			
12	Totals	€ 271.23	€ 60.28		€ 1,289.05		

dealing with percentages

It is also possible to display a number as a **percentage** (%).

If you enter numbers followed by a % sign, the data will be recognised as a percentage and the % sign will be displayed.

If you have a calculation, and you want the result to **display as a percentage**, rather than decimals, you would use the format options to change the way the result is displayed. For example, you may want to show the closing balance in the spreadsheet on the previous page as a percentage of the opening balance.

To do this, you would first insert an appropriate text description in cell D4 and then the formula =B4/B3 in cell E4 (see pages 10-12 for formulas) to calculate the closing balance divided by the opening balance.

The spreadsheet would then look like this (note top bar and cells D4 and E4):

E4			f_x	=B4/B3			
	A	B	C	D	E	F	
1	Bank transactions						
2							
3	Opening balance	€ 1,500.00					
4	Closing balance	€ 1,289.05		C.Bal/O.Bal	0.86		
5							
6	Date	Debit	Credit	Balance			
7	02/07/2014	€ 95.34	€ 0.00	€ 1,404.66			
8	11/07/2014	€ 0.00	€ 25.50	€ 1,430.16			
9	15/07/2014	€ 0.00	€ 34.78	€ 1,464.94			
10	22/07/2014	€ 67.90	€ 0.00	€ 1,397.04			
11	28/07/2014	€ 107.99	€ 0.00	€ 1,289.05			
12	Totals	€ 271.23	€ 60.28		€ 1,289.05		

To make cell E4 display as a **percentage**:

■ select the required cell

■ right click on the selection

■ select **Format cells**

■ select the **Number** tab

■ select category **Percentage**

■ adjust the decimal places as required

The spreadsheet will then appear as shown on the next page.

	E4		▾ ◉	*fx*	=B4/B3			⌄
◢	A	B	C	D	E	F		⌐
1	Bank transactions							▲
2								
3	Opening balance	€1,500.00						
4	Closing balance	€1,289.05		C.Bal/O.Bal	85.94%			≣
5								
6	Date	Debit	Credit	Balance				
7	02/07/2014	€95.34	€0.00	€1,404.66				
8	11/07/2014	€0.00	€25.50	€1,430.16				
9	15/07/2014	€0.00	€34.78	€1,464.94				
10	22/07/2014	€67.90	€0.00	€1,397.04				
11	28/07/2014	€107.99	€0.00	€1,289.05				
12	Totals	€271.23	€60.28		€1,289.05			▼

Note: applying a format of percentage will automatically multiply the selected cell (or cells) by 100 to create a percentage.

DATE FORMATS

dates

There are a variety of different ways in which dates can be displayed.

The common way of describing dates is to use 'd' for day, 'm' for month and 'y' for year.

If we take the date of 10th February 2010, it can be displayed in the following formats (for UK dates):

- dd/mm/yyyy would display as 10/02/2010
- dd/mm/yy would display as 10/02/10
- mm/dd/yy would display as 02/10/10

To change the way a date is displayed:

- select the required cells
- right click on the selection
- select **Format cells**
- select the **Number** tab
- select category **Date**
- choose the format you require from the drop-down list

The spreadsheet at the top of the next page shows the year date amended from 2014 to 14.

	A	B	C	D	E	F
1	Bank transactions					
2						
3	Opening balance	€ 1,500.00				
4	Closing balance	€ 1,289.05		C.Bal/O.Bal	85.94%	
5						
6	Date	Debit	Credit	Balance		
7	02/07/14	€ 95.34	€ 0.00	€ 1,404.66		
8	11/07/14	€ 0.00	€ 25.50	€ 1,430.16		
9	15/07/14	€ 0.00	€ 34.78	€ 1,464.94		
10	22/07/14	€ 67.90	€ 0.00	€ 1,397.04		
11	28/07/14	€ 107.99	€ 0.00	€ 1,289.05		
12	Totals	€ 271.23	€ 60.28		€ 1,289.05	

dates and time

Occasionally it is useful to include the time within a date, or even just to show the time on its own. There are specific formats to allow for this, within the format options.

The common way of describing times is to use 'h' for hour, 'm' for minutes and 's' for seconds.

The default time format is hh:mm:ss

For example, 40 seconds after half past one in the afternoon could be displayed as:

13:30:40

Or

01:30:40 PM

Additional date and time formats are available under the category **Custom**.

Current date and time – NOW()

Sometimes, it is useful to include the current date and time in a spreadsheet showing when it was last updated.

Every time the spreadsheet is re-opened, the date and time will be updated to the current date and time, and these values will be stored when the spreadsheet is saved.

There is a function specifically available to do this: **NOW()**

In our example on the next page, you can see that we have put =NOW() in cell D1, and then formatted the cell, to show the date, and just the hours and the minutes.

This is showing 9 minutes past 11 on the 4th of September 2014.

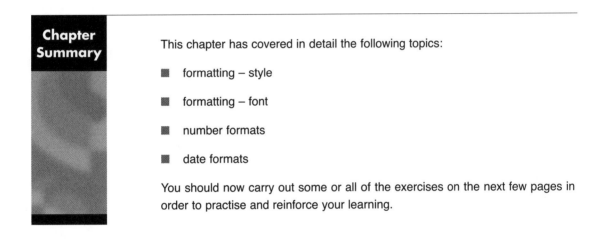

	A	B	C	D	E	F
1	Bank transactions			04/09/2014 11:09		
2						
3	Opening balance	€ 1,500.00				
4	Closing balance	€ 1,289.05		C.Bal/O.Bal	85.94%	
5						
6	Date	Debit	Credit	Balance		
7	02/07/14	€ 95.34	€ 0.00	€ 1,404.66		

Chapter Summary

This chapter has covered in detail the following topics:

■ formatting – style

■ formatting – font

■ number formats

■ date formats

You should now carry out some or all of the exercises on the next few pages in order to practise and reinforce your learning.

Activities

Exercise 1 – formatting practice

In this exercise we will open a spreadsheet created in an earlier exercise to practise some of the formatting described in this chapter.

Stage 1

1. Open the Bank transactions workbook Ch2Exercise1 created in the previous chapter (if not available, download the file Ch3Bank from www.osbornebooks.co.uk).

2. Save this workbook with the name **Ch3Exercise1**.

The worksheet should appear as shown below:

	A	B	C	D	E	F	
1	Bank transactions						
2							
3	Opening balance	1500					
4	Closing balance	1288.96					
5							
6	Date	Debit	Credit	Balance			
7	02/07/2014	95.34	0	1404.66			
8	11/07/2014	0	25.5	1430.16			
9	15/07/2014	0	34.78	1464.94			
10	22/07/2014	67.99	0	1396.95			
11	28/07/2014	107.99	0	1288.96			
12	Totals	271.32	60.28		1288.96		
13							

Sheet1 | **July** | Sheet3

3. Change the font **style** of Bank transactions (cell A1) to **bold**.

4. Change the font **size** of Bank transactions (cell A1) to 14.

5. Opening balance and Closing balance should be **style Italics** (cells B3,B4).

6. In cell E1, enter the formula to display today's date and time.

7. Format cell E1 to just display the time (hh:mm:ss).

8. All of the totals row (row 12) should be **bold**.

9. Make the column headings in row 6 **bold**.

10. Save your workbook with the name **Ch3Exercise1**.

Your workbook should appear as shown below, although the value in cell E1 will show your current time.

	A	B	C	D	E	F
1	**Bank transactions**				09:38:00	
2						
3	*Opening balance*	1500				
4	*Closing balance*	1288.96				
5						
6	**Date**	**Debit**	**Credit**	**Balance**		
7	02/07/2014	95.34	0	1404.66		
8	11/07/2014	0	25.5	1430.16		
9	15/07/2014	0	34.78	1464.94		
10	22/07/2014	67.99	0	1396.95		
11	28/07/2014	107.99	0	1288.96		
12	**Totals**	271.32	60.28		1288.96	

Sheet1　**July**　Sheet3

Stage 2

We will practise using some other formats:

1. Format the dates (cells C7 to C11) to display with two digits for the year, and with day, month, year separated by a . (full stop), rather than a / (forward slash).

2. Change the headings in row 6; **turn off bold**, and make them *italics* and **underlined**.

3. Format cells B3 and B4 to **currency, two decimal places**, with **currency symbol £**.

4. Format column E to **currency, two decimal places**, with **currency symbol £**.

   Notice how the time displayed in cell E1 changes to currency as well.

5. Use **Undo** to undo the formatting of column E (**Undo** is described in the preliminaries of chapter 1, page 3).

6. Format cell E12 to **currency, two decimal places**, with **currency symbol £**.

7. Save your worksheet.

Your workbook should appear as shown on the next page. As before, the value in cell E1 will show your current time.

	A	B	C	D	E	F
1	**Bank transactions**				10:13:59	
2						
3	*Opening balance*	£1,500.00				
4	*Closing balance*	£1,288.96				
5						
6	*Date*	*Debit*	*Credit*	*Balance*		
7	2.7.14	95.34	0	1404.66		
8	11.7.14	0	25.5	1430.16		
9	15.7.14	0	34.78	1464.94		
10	22.7.14	67.99	0	1396.95		
11	28.7.14	107.99	0	1288.96		
12	**Totals**	271.32	60.28		£1,288.96	

Sheet1 **July** Sheet3

Stage 3

In this stage we will complete our formatting:

1. Insert a row between rows 6 and 7.
2. In cells B7, C7 and D7 enter £ and make sure it is **underlined** in each cell.
3. Format cells B8 to B13 and C8 to C13 to display with **two decimal places**.
4. Format cells D8 to D12 to display with **two decimal places** and a **comma** for thousands.
5. **Double underline** the numbers in the Totals row (row 13).
6. Save your workbook.

The completed workbook can be seen below:

	A	B	C	D	E	F
1	**Bank transactions**				10:27:08	
2						
3	*Opening balance*	£1,500.00				
4	*Closing balance*	£1,288.96				
5						
6	*Date*	*Debit*	*Credit*	*Balance*		
7		£	£	£		
8	2.7.14	95.34	0.00	1,404.66		
9	11.7.14	0.00	25.50	1,430.16		
10	15.7.14	0.00	34.78	1,464.94		
11	22.7.14	67.99	0.00	1,396.95		
12	28.7.14	107.99	0.00	1,288.96		
13	**Totals**	271.32	60.28		£1,288.96	

Sheet1 **July** Sheet3

Exercise 2 – using percentages and decimal places

In this exercise we will create a simple spreadsheet to create the line-by-line detail for an invoice.

Stage 1

This stage is about creating the basic layout of our spreadsheet.

All text should be entered in the default typeface, font size 10, normal style.

1. Open a new workbook.
2. Move to **Sheet1**.
3. Rename the worksheet **Invoice 201**.
4. Starting in cell A1, enter the text as shown below to create the layout of the invoice.

Invoice Date:							
Customer No.:							
Product	Description	Qty	Price	Unit	Total	Discount	Net
Code			£		£	%	£

5. Widen column A so that all the text fits within the column.
6. Widen column B to 18.
7. Format the columns for Price, Total and Net as **Currency, £, two decimal places** (columns D, F and H).
8. Format discount % to **percentage** with **one decimal place**.
9. Save your workbook with the name **Ch3Exercise2**.

Your spreadsheet should look as shown below:

◢	A	B	C	D	E	F	G	H
1	Invoice Date:							
2								
3	Customer No.:							
4								
5	Product	Description	Qty	Price	Unit	Total	Discount	Net
6	Code			£		£	%	£
7								
8								
9								

Invoice 201 / Sheet2 / Sheet3

Stage 2

During this stage we will enter the product details for the invoice:

1. **Underline** Invoice Date and Customer No. (cells A1 and A3).

2. Enter **01/12/2014** for Invoice Date (cell B1).

3. Enter **1498** for Customer No.

4. Make the column headings in rows 5 and 6 **Bold**.

5. Enter the details of the products sold, as shown in the table below:

Product	Description	Qty	Price	Unit
PAPER-R	Paper - Ream	4	2.15	each
PEN-50	Pens box - 50	2	9.99	each
A4FOLD-3	A4 Ring Folder - 3	3	2.5	each
PAD-1	Lined pads - 1	6	1.7	each
ENVA4-100	Envelopes A4 - 100	3	10.99	each

6. Format the Price column (column D) to show **two decimal places** (no currency sign).

7. Save your workbook.

Your worksheet should look as shown below:

	A	B	C	D	E	F	G	H
1	Invoice Date:	01/12/2014						
2								
3	Customer No.:	1498						
4								
5	Product	Description	Qty	Price	Unit	Total	Discount	Net
6	Code			£		£	%	£
7	PAPER-R	Paper -Ream	4	2.15	each			
8	PEN-50	Pens box - 50	2	9.99	each			
9	A4FOLD-3	A4 Ring Folder - 3	3	2.50	each			
10	PAD-1	Lined pads - 1	6	1.70	each			
11	ENVA4-100	Envelopes A4 -100	3	10.99	each			
12								

Invoice 201 / Sheet2 / Sheet3

Stage 3

During this stage we are going to enter the formulas for Totals and Discount values:

1. In the Total column, cell F7, enter the formula to calculate the Total price for the Paper item (Qty * Price).

2. Enter the formulas for the Total for the remaining items.

3. Format the Total column (column F) to show **two decimal places** (no currency sign).

4. Format the Discount column (column G) to **percentage no decimal places**.

5. Enter Discount values of 5, 10, 5, 2 and 4 in cells G7 through to G11 respectively.

To help us do our calculations relating to the discount value, we are going to include an extra column on our invoice which would not normally be shown on an invoice. The calculation would usually be done in just one step, rather than two.

6. Insert a column between the Discount and the Net columns (G and H). This column is going to hold the calculated value of the discount.

7. In cell H5, enter **Discount**, and in cell H6, enter £.

8. Format the Discount £ column (column H) to show **two decimal places** (no currency sign).

9. In cell H7, enter the formula to calculate the Discount £ for the Paper item (Total * Discount %).

10. Enter the formulas for the Discount £ for the remaining items.

11. Save your workbook.

Your worksheet should look as shown below:

	A	B	C	D	E	F	G	H	I
1	Invoice Date:	01/12/2014							
2									
3	Customer No.:	1498							
4									
5	Product	Description	Qty	Price	Unit	Total	Discount	Discount	Net
6	Code			£		£	%	£	£
7	PAPER-R	Paper -Ream	4	2.15	each	8.60	5%	0.43	
8	PEN-50	Pens box - 50	2	9.99	each	19.98	10%	2.00	
9	A4FOLD-3	A4 Ring Folder - 3	3	2.50	each	7.50	5%	0.38	
10	PAD-1	Lined pads - 1	6	1.70	each	10.20	2%	0.20	
11	ENVA4-100	Envelopes A4 -100	3	10.99	each	32.97	4%	1.32	

Invoice 201 / Sheet2 / Sheet3

Stage 4

We are going complete the invoice in this stage:

1. In the Net column, cell I7, enter the formula to calculate the Net price for the Paper item (Total £ – Discount £).

2. Enter the formulas for the Net £ for the remaining items.

We are now going to total the invoice and add the VAT:

3. In cell H12, enter **Subtotal**, and in I12, enter the formula to total the Net Values (I7 to I11).

4. In cell H13, enter **VAT (20%)**, and in I13, enter the formula to calculate the VAT at 20% (=I12*20/100) or (=I12*0.2).

5. In cell H14, enter **TOTAL** and in cell I14, enter the formula to calculate the invoice TOTAL by adding the Subtotal and the VAT.

6. **Double underline** your TOTAL value (cell I14).

7. Having completed the invoice you see an error. Change the Qty of Envelopes to **6** (cell C11).

8. Also, change the Price for pens to **10.99** (cell D8).

9. Save your workbook.

Your worksheet should look as shown below:

	A	B	C	D	E	F	G	H	I
1	Invoice Date:	01/12/2014							
2									
3	Customer No.:	1498							
4									
5	Product	Description	Qty	Price	Unit	Total	Discount	Discount	Net
6	Code			£		£	%	£	£
7	PAPER-R	Paper -Ream	4	2.15	each	8.60	5%	0.43	8.17
8	PEN-50	Pens box - 50	2	10.99	each	21.98	10%	2.20	19.78
9	A4FOLD-3	A4 Ring Folder - 3	3	2.50	each	7.50	5%	0.38	7.13
10	PAD-1	Lined pads - 1	6	1.70	each	10.20	2%	0.20	10.00
11	ENVA4-100	Envelopes A4 -100	6	10.99	each	65.94	4%	2.64	63.30
12								Subtotal	108.38
13								VAT (20%)	21.68
14								TOTAL	130.05

Exercise 3 – using formatting and dates

In this exercise we will create a simple spreadsheet to record summary invoice details for a month.

Stage 1

This stage is about creating the basic layout of our spreadsheet.

All text should be entered in the default typeface, font size 10, normal style.

1. Open a new workbook.
2. Rename the worksheet Sheet1 to **Invoices**.
3. Using worksheet Invoices, enter **Invoice summary** in cell A1.
4. Enter **Date**, **Customer**, **Net**, **VAT**, **Gross**, and **Date Paid** in cells A2 through to F2 respectively.
5. Details for the first two invoices are as follows:

    01/12/2014, Farmhouse Foods, 122.99.

    09/12/2014, The Halal Centre, 238.90.

    Enter these details on rows 3 and 4.
6. Insert a row between rows 1 and 2 to create space below the title.
7. Widen column B (the customer column) to 20.
8. Save your worksheet with the name **Ch3Exercise3**.

Your worksheet should look as shown below:

	A	B	C	D	E	F
1	Invoice summary					
2						
3	Date	Customer	Net	VAT	Gross	Date Paid
4	01/12/2014	Farmhouse Foods	122.99			
5	09/12/2014	The Halal Centre	238.9			
6						
7						
8						
9						
10						
11						

Invoices / Sheet2 / Sheet3

Stage 2

We are now going to apply some formatting, and enter more invoices:

1. Continue with workbook **Ch3Exercise3**.

2. Enter the invoices from the table as shown below:

Date	Customer	Net
11/12/2014	W B Meats	218.95
13/12/2014	Edwards Farm	95.45
15/12/2014	T F Curries	317.99
20/12/2014	Ahmed Foods	67.50

3. Format the Net column (column C), as **Currency £**, with **two decimal places**.

4. Change the font size of Invoice summary (cell A1) to 14.

5. Change the format of the Date column (A) to show just two digits for the year.

6. Save your workbook.

Your worksheet should now look as shown below:

	A	B	C	D	E	F
1	Invoice summary					
2						
3	Date	Customer	Net	VAT	Gross	Date Paid
4	01/12/14	Farmhouse Foods	£122.99			
5	09/12/14	The Halal Centre	£238.90			
6	11/12/14	W B Meats	£218.95			
7	13/12/14	Edwards Farm	£95.45			
8	15/12/14	T F Curries	£317.99			
9	20/12/14	Ahmed Foods	£67.50			
10						
11						
12						

Invoices / Sheet2 / Sheet3

Stage 3

1. We have missed some invoices.

   Enter the invoices from the table as shown below between rows 4 and 5 to keep the invoices in date order.

Date	Customer	Net
4/12/2014	Fast Foods	56.95
5/12/2014	The Snack Bar	195.45

2. Make each of the column headings in row 3, **bold** and **underlined**.

3. In cell A12, enter the text **Totals** in **bold**.

4. Enter the formula in C12 to total the Net figures.

5. We are now going to calculate the VAT element for each of these invoices, based on a VAT rate of 20%.

   Create the formula in cell D4 =C4*20/100 or =C4*0.2.

6. Copy this formula to cells D5 through to D11.

7. Now for the Gross figures, the value of the Net + the VAT:

   Create the formula in cell E4 (=C4+D4).

8. Copy this formula to cells E5 through to E11.

9. Now total the VAT and Gross values in cells D12 and E12 (copy the totals formula from C12 to D12 and E12).

10. **Double underline** and make **bold** the totals values.

11. Save your workbook.

Your worksheet should now look as follows:

	A	B	C	D	E	F
1	Invoice summary					
2						
3	**Date**	**Customer**	**Net**	**VAT**	**Gross**	**Date Paid**
4	01/12/14	Farmhouse Foods	£122.99	£24.60	£147.59	
5	04/12/14	Fast Foods	£56.95	£11.39	£68.34	
6	05/12/14	The Snack Bar	£195.45	£39.09	£234.54	
7	09/12/14	The Halal Centre	£238.90	£47.78	£286.68	
8	11/12/14	W B Meats	£218.95	£43.79	£262.74	
9	13/12/14	Edwards Farm	£95.45	£19.09	£114.54	
10	15/12/14	T F Curries	£317.99	£63.60	£381.59	
11	20/12/14	Ahmed Foods	£67.50	£13.50	£81.00	
12	**Totals**		**£1,314.18**	**£262.84**	**£1,577.02**	

Invoices / Sheet2 / Sheet3 /

The formulas can be seen in the image below:

B	C	D	E
Customer	**Net**	**VAT**	**Gross**
Farmhouse Foods	122.99	=C4*20/100	=C4+D4
Fast Foods	56.95	=C5*20/100	=C5+D5
The Snack Bar	195.45	=C6*20/100	=C6+D6
The Halal Centre	238.9	=C7*20/100	=C7+D7
W B Meats	218.95	=C8*20/100	=C8+D8
Edwards Farm	95.45	=C9*20/100	=C9+D9
T F Curries	317.99	=C10*20/100	=C10+D10
Ahmed Foods	67.5	=C11*20/100	=C11+D11
	=SUM(C4:C11)	=SUM(D4:D11)	=SUM(E4:E11)

Stage 4

We will make some final edits in this stage to both the format and the invoices:

1. Change the date for the Fast Foods invoice to **03/12/14**.
2. The Net value for the Ahmed Foods invoice should be **£167.50**, make the change.
3. We have some information about the dates on which some of the invoices have been paid.

Date	Customer	Date Paid
1/12/14	Farmhouse Foods	22/12/14
5/12/14	The Snack Bar	06/12/14
15/12/14	T F Curries	15/12/14

Enter the Date Paid values for these invoices.

4. Change the format of the Date Paid column (F) to show four digits for the year, if it is not already showing four digits.
5. For all those invoices which have been paid, change all details to font style **Italics**.
6. For those invoices which have not been paid, change the Gross figures to colour **Red**.
7. Save your workbook.

Your worksheet should look as shown on the next page:

	A	B	C	D	E	F
1	Invoice summary					
2						
3	Date	Customer	Net	VAT	Gross	Date Paid
4	01/12/14	Farmhouse Foods	£122.99	£24.60	£147.59	22/12/2014
5	03/12/14	Fast Foods	£56.95	£11.39	£68.34	
6	05/12/14	The Snack Bar	£195.45	£39.09	£234.54	06/12/2014
7	09/12/14	The Halal Centre	£238.90	£47.78	£286.68	
8	11/12/14	W B Meats	£218.95	£43.79	£262.74	
9	13/12/14	Edwards Farm	£95.45	£19.09	£114.54	
10	15/12/14	T F Curries	£317.99	£63.60	£381.59	15/12/2014
11	20/12/14	Ahmed Foods	£167.50	£33.50	£201.00	
12	Totals		£1,414.18	£282.84	£1,697.02	

Invoices / Sheet2 / Sheet3

4 Functions

this chapter covers...

In this chapter we are going to look at functions in more detail, showing how you can make use of some of the built-in calculation facilities, we will also cover the storage of your workbooks and look at different ways of printing.

When you have finished this chapter and carried out the exercises which follow, you should be able to use functions in your formulas, and be comfortable with file handling and printing.

The concepts and techniques covered are:

- *formulas – extending*

- *functions – definitions*

- *some useful statistical functions*

- *file handling*

- *printing and page setup*

FORMULAS

As we have seen in previous chapters, whenever we wish to carry out a calculation or enter a formula into a cell within our spreadsheet, we move to the cell where we want the formula to appear and start by entering an equal sign =.

mathematical operators

As mentioned previously, the common mathematical operators which we will use in our formulas, are as follows:-

- Addition: +

- Subtraction: –

- Multiplication: *

- Division: /

Formulas make use of brackets: ( )

As with our normal mathematics there is an order that will be followed when a formula is interpreted, known as the operator precedence.

The order of calculations within any formula is as follows:

- any calculation contained in brackets is done first

- division and multiplication are ranked the same

- addition and subtraction are ranked the same

So, if we want to group parts of our calculation to ensure that certain parts are calculated before a subsequent part, then we would use brackets.

Some examples:

=(B3+B4+15)/100

Here B3 and B4 and 15 are added together and the result is divided by 100.

This gives a very different result to:

=(B3+B4)+15/100

Here 15 is divided by 100 and the result is added to the sum of B3 and B4.

Brackets are very important in the construction of formulas.

formulas – selecting cells

In previous examples, when we have created a formula, we have manually entered the reference for a cell; this can be made simpler and quicker by just clicking on the required cell(s) as we enter the formula. Each cell selection is followed by typing the mathematical operator we wish to apply, or **ENTER** when we have completed the formula.

For example in the costing spreadsheet below, if we want to enter a formula for the total unit cost, in cell C10, (which would be the Total Cost (C9) divided by the No of Units (B3)), follow the steps below:

	C10			f_x				
	A	B	C	D	E	F	G	
1	Production costs							
2								
3	No of Units	12000			18000			
4								
5		Unit Cost	Total Cost		Unit Cost	Total Cost		
6	Materials	£5	£60,000		£5	£90,000		
7	Labour	£2	£24,000		£2	£36,000		
8	Fixed Costs	£3.00	£36,000		£2.00	£36,000		
9	Total	£10	£120,000		£9	£162,000		
10	Total Unit Cost							

Sheet1 / Sheet2 / Sheet3

- select cell C10
- enter = (the equals sign)
- click on cell C9

The C9 cell is highlighted and the formula starts to appear in the formula bar, as shown below:

	SUM		X ✓	f_x =C9				
	A	B	C	D	E	F	G	
1	Production costs							
2								
3	No of Units	12000			18000			
4								
5		Unit Cost	Total Cost		Unit Cost	Total Cost		
6	Materials	£5	£60,000		£5	£90,000		
7	Labour	£2	£24,000		£2	£36,000		
8	Fixed Costs	£3.00	£36,000		£2.00	£36,000		
9	Total	£10	£120,000		£9	£162,000		
10	Total Unit Cost		=C9					

Sheet1 / Sheet2 / Sheet3

■ enter / (forward slash for division)

■ click on cell B3

You can see the required formula, in the formula bar.

	SUM	▼	× ✓ fx	=C9/B3			▼
	A	B	C	D	E	F	G
1	Production costs						
2							
3	No of Units	12000			18000		
4							
5		Unit Cost	Total Cost		Unit Cost	Total Cost	
6	Materials	£5	£60,000		£5	£90,000	
7	Labour	£2	£24,000		£2	£36,000	
8	Fixed Costs	£3.00	£36,000		£2.00	£36,000	
9	Total	£10	£120,000		£9	£162,000	
10	Total Unit Cost		=C9/B3				

Sheet1 / Sheet2 / Sheet3

■ press **ENTER** to show the formula is complete

	C10	▼	fx	=C9/B3			▼
	A	B	C	D	E	F	G
1	Production costs						
2							
3	No of Units	12000			18000		
4							
5		Unit Cost	Total Cost		Unit Cost	Total Cost	
6	Materials	£5	£60,000		£5	£90,000	
7	Labour	£2	£24,000		£2	£36,000	
8	Fixed Costs	£3.00	£36,000		£2.00	£36,000	
9	Total	£10	£120,000		£9	£162,000	
10	Total Unit Cost		£10				

Sheet1 / Sheet2 / Sheet3

This will speed up the creation of formulas.

Here is another very useful technique, relating to the formula bar:

■ click on a cell containing a formula – the formula is displayed in the formula bar

■ click into the formula bar – all the cells included in the formula are highlighted

■ to exit without making any changes to the formula, press **ESC** (see image on the next page)

| SUM | ▾ | X ✓ fx | =B4+B5+B6+B7+B8 | | | ▾ |

◢	A	B	C	D	E	F	G
1	Hours worked						
2							
3	Week Beg	1st Apr	8th Apr	15th Apr	22nd Apr	29th Apr	
4	Mon	6	7	7	8	6.5	
5	Tue	7.5	6.5	7	7.5	7.5	
6	Wed	5	7.5	7	6	8	
7	Thu	7	6.5	6.5	7.5	7	
8	Fri	8	7.5	7.5	5	8	
9							
10	Totals	=B4+B5+B(					

MORE ON FUNCTIONS

As discussed previously, spreadsheet packages contain built-in formulas called Functions that make it easy to perform common calculations on data. We have made use of the **SUM** function **=SUM( )** to add up values.

Most functions are designed to accept data which is then used in the calculations, but not all as we saw with the **NOW()** function, which just gives us the current time and date each time we open a workbook.

As we have seen, in functions which perform calculations on our data, the data is entered within the round brackets which follow the function's name such as:

=SUM(A1,A2,A3)

To repeat the key points relating to functions:

The values within the round brackets are known as 'arguments' with each argument (or value) separated from the previous argument (value) by a comma.

The **type** of argument will vary from function to function: it could be a number, or a cell reference, or group of cells.

The **number** of arguments may also vary from function to function.

If an argument is **optional** (i.e. you don't have to enter it) you will see the argument in square brackets, for example [number2].

The result which a function creates is said to be the value **returned** by the function, and is known as the **return value**.

ranges

As we have seen, a range is a **group or block of cells in a worksheet**. It is a shorthand way of specifying the first and last cell and automatically including all the cells inbetween.

To reiterate, a range is identified by the cell reference of the first cell (upper left cell), followed by a colon, then the cell reference of the last cell (bottom right). Examples of a range of cells include:

D4:D11 – all the cells are in the same column

C4:F4 – all the cells are in the same row

B4:F8 – a block of cells across several rows and columns, as can be seen highlighted in the example below.

B4				f_x	6		
	A	B	C	D	E	F	G
1	Hours worked						
2							
3	Week Beg	1st Apr	8th Apr	15th Apr	22nd Apr	29th Apr	
4	Mon	6	7	7	8	6.5	
5	Tue	7.5	6.5	7	7.5	7.5	
6	Wed	5	7.5	7	6	8	
7	Thu	7	6.5	6.5	7.5	7	
8	Fri	8	7.5	7.5	5	8	
9							

A:A – all cells in a column A

3:3 – all cells in row 3

A range of cells as described above can be used as an argument within a function, for example **=SUM(B:B)** to sum all cells in column B.

SUM

We have already looked at and used the **SUM** function. The formal description (often called the definition) is given below:

The **SUM** function adds all the numbers that you specify as arguments.

Each argument can be a number, a cell reference, a range of cells, or the result of another function:

=SUM(number1, [number2], [number3],...)

The **SUM** function has these arguments:

- number1 is required
- number2, number3 . . . are optional

You can specify up to a total of 255 arguments (values) to be added together.

For example:

=SUM(C2,C16,C20)

This would return the sum of the numbers in the cells C2, C16, and C20.

SUM is often used for a **range of cells**, for example:

=SUM(B2:B18)

This would return the sum of all the numbers in the range B2 to B18, ie cells

B2,B3,B4 etc... all the way to B18.

The screen illustrated below uses the formula **=SUM(B4:B8,172)** to total all five weeks of daily work bookings, and add a value of 172 (the hours for the previous month). This produces a total of 346.5.

G10	▼	fx	=SUM(B4:F8,172)					
	A	B	C	D	E	F	G	
2								
3	Week Beg	1st Apr	8th Apr	15th Apr	22nd Apr	29th Apr		
4	Mon	6	7	7	8	6.5		
5	Tue	7.5	6.5	7	7.5	7.5		
6	Wed	5	7.5	7	6	8		
7	Thu	7	6.5	6.5	7.5	7		
8	Fri	8	7.5	7.5	5	8		
9								
10	Totals	33.5					346.5	

SOME MORE USEFUL FUNCTIONS

The functions we are going to cover in this chapter are as follows:

- COUNT
- MAX
- MIN
- AVERAGE

count

The **COUNT** function counts the **number of cells that contain numbers** within a group of cells specified by the user. The formula is:

=COUNT(value1,[value2],...)

The **COUNT** function has these arguments:

■ **value1**

This is required and can be the first item, cell reference, or range within which you want to count numbers.

■ **value2**

This is optional.

You can specify up to 255 arguments. Each 'argument' can be either a number, cell reference, or range of cells.

Here are some examples:

=COUNT(B1:B16)

This would tell us how many cells in the range B1 to B16 contain numbers.

=COUNT(B1:B16,C20:C36)

This would return the total of how many cells in the range B1 to B16 and C20 to C36 contain numbers.

A simple illustration is shown in the screen image below, where we have an exam results spreadsheet, showing the results for five students across four modules.

We are using the **COUNT** function to tell us how many exams each person took, this is shown in the **Exams Taken** column.

The formula **=COUNT(B4:E4)** is entered in cell F4 to tell us how many exams John Smith sat. This formula is then copied to the remaining student rows.

	F4		f_x	=COUNT(B4:E4)			
	A	B	C	D	E	F	
1	Midterm exams						
2						Exams	
3	Name	Module1	Module2	Module3	Module4	Taken	
4	John Smith	75%	62%	45%	65%	4	
5	Harpret Bhopal	61%	48%			2	
6	Wendy Owen	63%	80%	51%	41%	4	
7	Mohammed Iqbal	53%		41%	64%	3	
8	Barbara White	42%	63%	85%	43%	4	

MAX

'**MAX**' is an abbreviation of 'maximum'. The **MAX** function returns the maximum (largest) number within a group of cells specified by the user.

The formula is:

=MAX(number1,number2,...)

The **MAX** function has these arguments:

■ **number1** – this is required

■ **number2** – this is optional

You can specify up to 255 arguments for which you want to find the maximum value. Each argument can be either a number, cell reference, or range.

Here are some examples:

=MAX(B1:B6)

This would return the largest of the numbers in the range B1 to B6.

=MAX(B1:B6,80)

This would return the largest of the numbers in the range B1 to B6, and 80, ie if none of the numbers within the range is greater than 80 it would return a value of 80.

In the exam results spreadsheet shown below, we have set up Row 10 to show the maximum (highest) mark for each of the four modules. The formula is input in B10 and copied to cells C10, D10 and E10.

B10			f_x	=MAX(B4:B8)			
	A	B	C	D	E	F	
1	Midterm exams						
2						Exams	
3	**Name**	**Module1**	**Module2**	**Module3**	**Module4**	**Taken**	
4	John Smith	75%	62%	45%	65%	4	
5	Harpret Bhopal	61%	48%			2	
6	Wendy Owen	63%	80%	51%	41%	4	
7	Mohammed Iqbal	53%		41%	64%	3	
8	Barbara White	42%	63%	85%	43%	4	
9							
10	Max	75%	80%	85%	65%		

MIN

'**MIN**' is an abbreviation of 'minimum'. The **MIN** function returns the smallest number within a group of cells specified by the user.

The formula is

=MIN(number1,number2,...)

The **MIN** function has these arguments:

- **number1** – this is required
- **number2** – this is optional

You can specify up to 255 arguments for which you want to find the minimum value. Each argument can be either a number, or cell reference, or range.

Here are some examples:

=MIN(C2:C16)

This would return the smallest of the numbers in the range C2 to C16.

=MIN(C2:C16,10)

This would return the smallest of the numbers in the range C2 to C16, and 10, ie if none of the numbers within the range is smaller than 10 it would return a value of 10.

In the exam results spreadsheet shown below, we have this time set up Row 10 to show the minimum (lowest) mark for each of the four modules. The formula has been input in B10 and copied to cells C10, D10 and E10.

	B10	▼	f_x	=MIN(B4:B8)		
	A	B	C	D	E	F
1	Midterm exams					
2						Exams
3	Name	Module1	Module2	Module3	Module4	Taken
4	John Smith	75%	62%	45%	65%	4
5	Harpret Bhopal	61%	48%			2
6	Wendy Owen	63%	80%	51%	41%	4
7	Mohammed Iqbal	53%		41%	64%	3
8	Barbara White	42%	63%	85%	43%	4
9						
10	Min	42%	80%	85%	65%	

AVERAGE

The **AVERAGE** function returns the average (arithmetic mean) of a group of cells specified by the user.

The formula is:

=AVERAGE(number1,number2,...)

The **AVERAGE** function has these arguments:

- **number1** – this is required
- **number2** – this is optional

You can specify up to 255 arguments for which you want to find the **AVERAGE** value. Each argument can be either a number, or cell reference, or range.

Here are some examples:

=AVERAGE(A2:C16)

This would return the average of the numbers in the cell range C2 to C16.

=AVERAGE(C2:C16,10)

This would return the average of the numbers in the cell range C2 to C16 and 10.

In the exam results spreadsheet shown below, we have this time set up Row 10 to show the Average (arithmetic mean) mark for each of the four modules. The formula **=AVERAGE(B4:B8)** has been input in B10 and copied to cells C10, D10 and E10.

	E10	▼	f_x	=AVERAGE(E4:E8)		
	A	B	C	D	E	F
1	Midterm exams					
2						Exams
3	Name	Module1	Module2	Module3	Module4	Taken
4	John Smith	75%	62%	45%	65%	4
5	Harpret Bhopal	61%	48%			2
6	Wendy Owen	63%	80%	51%	41%	4
7	Mohammed Iqbal	53%		41%	64%	3
8	Barbara White	42%	63%	85%	43%	4
9						
10	Average	59%	63%	56%	53%	

MORE ON FILES AND FOLDERS

Each workbook is held as one file. A file is the computer equivalent of a paper document containing the information which you have entered. Each file has a name which you specify when it is created. This should be chosen to be meaningful and help identify what the file contains, for example Timesheet Week14.

For spreadsheets which are updated on a regular basis, it can be useful to add a version number or part of a date to the filename so that different versions can be saved as the spreadsheet evolves. To save with a different name, you would use **Save As** described below.

Save As

To save a copy of the workbook with a different name either as a backup or as a fresh starting point, you would use **Save As** usually found under the File menu and supply a new name for the copy of the workbook.

This also allows a previous version to be identified and opened, if required.

close

When you have finished working on a spreadsheet, but do not wish to exit the spreadsheet program, you would close the workbook. There are several ways of doing this:

- select **Close** from the **File** menu
- click on the standard **x** in the top right of the workbook window frame

If you have made changes which you have not saved, you will be prompted to save them as you close the workbook.

folders

To organise our files in a logical way we store related files in a **folder**, which we name when we create it, this name should identify the type of files/documents the folder will contain. For example: Timesheets.

Within Excel the File and Folder tools mentioned below are available whenever you select one of the menu options such as **OPEN** or **SAVE AS** which are located under the **File** menu.

create a folder

Creating a folder can be achieved by using the **New Folder** option, and naming the folder appropriately.

finding a file

To find a previously saved workbook, you would either select **Open** from the **File** menu, navigate to the required folder and select the required workbook from the appropriate folder, or if it is listed, select the workbook from the list of recently used documents. If you are unable to locate the required workbook you can use the **Search tool** provided when you select **Open** within the **File** menu.

renaming a file

To rename a file, locate the file within your folders, click the filename, once then once more and type in the new name. Press **RETURN** or click somewhere else to complete the edit. **ESC** will cancel the edit.

sharing a file

To allow the sharing of a file across a network, the file needs to be in a folder which is accessible to other people on the network. By right mouse clicking on the folder name, and setting the **share with** options as required, you can specify who can access the file, or you may place the file in your Shared Documents folder if you are working with Windows®. It is likely that you will require assistance from your network supervisor to share files.

USB devices

To save a copy of your workbook to a removable device such as a USB stick, you would insert the device into a USB port on your computer, select **Save As**, and in the very left pane you should see a list of folders. Scrolling down this pane, you should see your Local Disk (C:), followed by other disk drives and devices, select the USB device, enter the appropriate **File name**, select **Save**.

backup off site

For security purposes a copy of an important workbook should be saved to removable media such as a USB stick and stored off site.

PAGE SETUP AND PRINTING

print preview

Once we have created and formatted our spreadsheet it is quite possible that we will want to print it.

Spreadsheets are not like word-processed documents – they do not automatically fit within one horizontal page width and flow on downwards.

The first step is to see what the spreadsheet would look like when printed, without actually printing. From the **File** menu, select **Print**. You will then see all the print settings which you can change, together with a **Print Preview** of the worksheet on the right hand side of the screen. Alternatively, you can select **Page Setup** from the **Page Layout** menu, then **Print Preview**.

print settings

If you need to make adjustments to the layout for printing, this can be done through **Settings** within the **Print** option, or through **Page Setup**.

These options allow you to:

- change the **orientation** – the default orientation is usually **Portrait** (taller than wide), so if the spreadsheet is slightly too wide to fit on one page width, you might change the orientation to **Landscape** (wider than tall)

- adjust the **Margins** – the amount of space to be left around the edges of your printing. It is possible to change margins for the top, bottom, left and right. You might want to reduce these to a minimum to give as much space as possible for printing your worksheet

- select **Scaling** – you can specify how many pages wide, by how many pages tall you want to fit the spreadsheet into; the most common is **Fit Sheet on one page** – where the spreadsheet is scaled to fit entirely on one page. Other alternatives are **Fit all columns on one page** and **Fit all rows on one page**. You would choose the option most suited to the size of your worksheet, but it is important to make sure that the text of the worksheet remains legible

There are other options available such as **Paper size**, and **Collated** which you can change.

Within **Page Setup**, you can also:

- check the **gridlines** box if you want to see gridlines for the rows and columns included on your printout

The two images below show print previews where the page orientations are:

■ portrait – taller than it is wider – like a portrait picture

■ landscape – wider than it is taller – like a landscape painting

The image below shows a print preview where the page orientation is **Portrait**.

The image below shows a print preview where the page orientation is **Landscape**.

headers and footers

It is sometimes useful to add a **header** or a **footer** to your spreadsheet. As you would expect a **header** is something which will usually appear at the top of each page when printed, this could be something like 'Company Confidential' and the date.

A **footer** will appear at the bottom and is often used to include the author and a page number if the printing covers more than one page.

To create a header or a footer:

■ select **Page Setup**

■ select **Header/Footer**

■ either select one of the built in choices from the drop down list for the header or footer such as page number or date

■ or create your own custom piece of text

An example **Header**, selected from the list is shown in the screen below:

Page	Margins	Header/Footer	Sheet	

Confidential   09/09/2014   Page 1

Header:

Confidential, 09/09/2014, Page 1   ▼

Custom Header...   Custom Footer...

An example **Footer**, selected from the list is shown in the screen below:

Footer:

Results, Page 1   ▼

                                         Results   Page 1

There are a number of additional items which can be inserted into either a header or a footer, these are available if you select **Custom** for your header or footer, and then pick the items you want and where you want to position them:

■ text

■ time

■ filename

■ picture

This can be seen in the image on the next page:

Header

To format text: select the text, then choose the Format Text button.
To insert a page number, date, time, file path, filename, or tab name: position the
  insertion point in the edit box, then choose the appropriate button.
To insert picture: press the Insert Picture button. To format your picture, place the
  cursor in the edit box and press the Format Picture button.

| A | | | | | | | | | |

Left section:	Center section:	Right section:
Confidential	&[Date]	Page &[Page]

---

page break

If we wish to format our printed output so that part of the information is on one page and the remainder on another page, we can insert what is known as a **page break**.

To insert a page break:

■ select the **Page Layout** menu

■ click on the cell to be the start of the new page

■ select **Breaks**

■ select **Insert Page Break**

Chapter Summary

This chapter has covered in detail the following topics:

■ formulas – extending

■ functions – definitions

■ some useful statistical functions

■ file handling

■ printing and page setup

You should now carry out some or all of the exercises on the next few pages in order to practise and reinforce your learning.

Activities

Exercise 1 – using functions

In this exercise we will download a spreadsheet containing some share prices, and make use of some of the simple statistical functions covered in this chapter.

Stage 1

1. Download the workbook **Ch4Shares**.

2. Open the downloaded file, save this workbook with the name **Ch4Exercise1** (using Save As).

The workbook should appear as shown below:

◢	A	B	C	D	E	F	G
1	**Share Price**						
2	226.7						
3	229.25						
4	226.15						
5	224.95						
6	225						
7	231.5						
8	228.6						
9	225.1						
10	223.85						

3. In cell D1 enter the text **All**, make it bold.

4. In cell C2 enter the text **Count**, make it bold.

5. In cell D2 enter the formula to display how many share prices there are in column A.

6. In cell C3 enter the text **Average**, make it bold.

7. In cell D3 enter the formula to display the average of the share prices there are in column A.

8. In cell C4 enter the text **Min**, make it bold.

9. In cell D4 enter the formula to display the minimum share price in column A.

10. In cell C5 enter the text **Max**, make it bold.

11. In cell D5 enter the formula to display the maximum share price in column A.

12. Save your workbook as **Ch4Exercise1**.

	A	B	C	D	E	F	G
1	Share Price			All			
2	226.7		Count	20			
3	229.25		Average	224.4825			
4	226.15		Min	218.85			
5	224.95		Max	231.5			
6	225						
7	231.5						
8	228.6						
9	225.1						
10	223.85						

The formulas are shown below.

Note: In this instance we have chosen to use the whole column as our range, since the only values in the column are share prices, we could also have used A2:A21.

	A	B	C	D
1	Share Price			All
2	226.7		Count	=COUNT(A:A)
3	229.25		Average	=AVERAGE(A:A)
4	226.15		Min	=MIN(A:A)
5	224.95		Max	=MAX(A:A)
6	225			
7	231.5			
8	228.6			
9	225.1			
10	223.85			

Stage 2

We are now going to calculate the same results by selecting the cells to use in the formulas.

1. Continue working with **Ch4Exercise1**.

2. In cell E1 enter **All (by range)**, make it bold.

3. In cell E2 enter the formula to display how many share prices there are in column A, by selecting the range of cells.

4. Repeat for each of Average, Min and Max and enter the formulas in cells E3 - E5 respectively.

5. Save your workbook.

The results in column E should be exactly the same as column D, an example formula is shown on the next page.

E5			f_x	=MAX(A2:A21)		
	A	B	C	D	E	F	G
1	**Share Price**			**All**	**All (by range)**		
2	226.7		**Count**	20	20		
3	229.25		**Average**	224.4825	224.4825		
4	226.15		**Min**	218.85	218.85		
5	224.95		**Max**	231.5	231.5		
6	225						
7	231.5						
8	228.6						
9	225.1						
10	223.85						
11	224.9						

That completes exercise 1.

Exercise 2 – more formulas

In this exercise we are going to practise using the mathematical operators in calculations including the use of brackets in an inventory count spreadsheet.

Stage 1

In this stage we are going to create our basic spreadsheet to record inventory levels of a number of products which are held in several different locations.

1. Open a new workbook.

2. In cell A1 enter **Inventory count,** make this bold and font size 14.

3. In cell A2 enter **Product code**.

4. In B2 enter **Location1**.

5. In C2 enter **Location2**.

6. In D2 enter **Price**.

7. Adjust the column widths so that all text from row 3 onwards fits in each cell.

8. Insert a row between rows 1 and 2 to give a space between the title and column headings.

9. Make the column headings bold and underlined.

10. Name the sheet WarehouseA.

11. Save the workbook with the name **Ch4Exercise2**.

Your layout should look as shown on the next page.

◢	A	B	C	D	E	F	⊟
1	**Inventory count**						
2							
3	**Product code**	**Location1**	**Location2**	**Price**			
4							
5							
6							
7							
8							
9							

|◄ ◄ ► ►| **WarehouseA** Sheet2 Sheet3 ◄ |

Stage 2

We are going to enter the details from the inventory count.

1. Enter the details from the inventory count as shown in the table below.

Product code	Location1	Location2	Price
ab1	241	357	2.5
ab2	1256	903	3.25
ab3	875	271	0.99
ab4	20974	15189	0.45
ab11	6523	298	1.37

2. Format the price column to **euros** with 2 decimal places.

3. In cell E3 enter **Value** (bold and underlined).

We are now going to calculate the total value of the inventory from the two locations.

4. Enter a formula in cell E4 to give the total value of the products from location1 and location2, using the price in cell D4. Note – you will need to use brackets.

5. Enter formulas for the value for each of the other product codes in cells E5 to E8 respectively.

6. Format the Value column to euros, with no decimal places.

7. Save your workbook.

The screen should look as shown on the next page.

	A	B	C	D	E	F
	E4			fx	=(B4+C4)*D4	
1	**Inventory count**					
2						
3	**Product code**	**Location1**	**Location2**	**Price**	**Value**	
4	ab1	241	357	€2.50	€1,495	
5	ab2	1256	903	€3.25	€7,017	
6	ab3	875	271	€0.99	€1,135	
7	ab4	20974	15189	€0.45	€16,273	
8	ab11	6523	298	€1.37	€9,345	
9						

WarehouseA / Sheet2 / Sheet3

Stage 3

We are going to make some changes to the details from the inventory count.

1. Enter the details from the inventory count as shown in the table below.

2. The price for product ab11 should be **€1.35**, make the change.

3. A recount has shown **15192** for product ab4 in location2.

4. Details have now come in for a third location. Insert a column between Location2 and Price, name it Location3, and enter quantities for the products as shown below:

Product code	Location3
ab1	1056
ab2	159
ab3	3715
ab4	11238
ab11	5211

5. Modify the formulas in the value column to include the Location3 quantities.

6. Two more products have now been counted, insert the details as shown below, between products ab4, and ab11.

Product code	Location1	Location2	Location3	Price
ab8	145	859	1023	€3.29
ab10	3256	1103	45	€2.25

7. Enter the appropriate formulas in the Value column for these two products.

8. We are now going to total the Values for all of the products. In Cell A11, enter **Total Value**, make it bold.

9. In cell F11, enter the formula to total all of the Values, make it bold and double underline.

10. Save your workbook.

Your workbook should look as shown below:

F4			f_x	=(B4+C4+D4)*E4		
	A	B	C	D	E	F
1	**Inventory count**					
2						
3	**Product code**	**Location1**	**Location2**	**Location3**	**Price**	**Value**
4	ab1	241	357	1056	€2.50	€4,135
5	ab2	1256	903	159	€3.25	€7,534
6	ab3	875	271	3715	€0.99	€4,812
7	ab4	20974	15192	11238	€0.45	€21,332
8	ab8	145	859	1023	€3.29	€6,669
9	ab10	3256	1103	45	€2.25	€9,909
10	ab11	6523	298	5211	€1.35	€16,243
11	**Total Value**					**€70,634**
12						

WarehouseA / Sheet2 / Sheet3

You have now completed exercise 2.

Exercise 3 – file handling

In this exercise, we are going to practise some file handling techniques.

Stage 1

We are going to use the workbook created in the last exercise.

1. Open the file **Ch4Exercise2** created in the previous exercise (if you do not have this file, it can be downloaded as described previously).

2. Save this file with a new name **Ch4Exercise3** in a new folder called **Working Folder**.

3. **Close** the workbook.

4. Select **File**, **Open**, and using the standard file/folder options, rename the file to **Ch4Exercise3.1**, and open the file **Ch4Exercise3.1**.

Note: you cannot change the name of a workbook if that workbook is open in your spreadsheet program.

Stage 2

In this stage, the specific actions needed will vary depending on your environment and you may need assistance form your network supervisor.

1. Save the workbook **Ch4Exercise3.1** to a USB memory stick or similar.

2. Find out how to share this workbook in your own environment.

Exercise 4 – printing

Stage 1

1. Download the file **Ch4Printing**.

2. Save the file as **Ch4Exercise4**.

3. Select **Print** and **Preview** your layout. You can see that the current layout will print on four pages, from the page selector at the bottom of the screen.

4. Change the orientation to **Landscape**. You can see that the current layout will now print on two pages, from the page selector at the bottom of the screen.

5. Change the **Scaling** to fit Sheet on One Page.

6. Change the orientation back to **Portrait**.

7. Using **Page setup**, create a **custom header** containing the text **Inventory Valuation Widgets** to the far right.

8. Create a **footer** with **page number** on the left and **today's date** to the right.

9. Print the worksheet.

10. Save your workbook.

The top of your printout should look as shown below:

								Inventory **Valuation Widgets**	

Stock take

Product code	Location1	Location2	Location3	Location4	Location5	Location6	Location7	Price	Value
ab1	241	357	1056	55	790	1056	524	€2.50	€10,198
ab2	1256	903	159	1056	45	159	79	€3.25	€11,885
ab3	875	271	3715	159	1056	3715	1056	€0.99	€10,739
ab4	20974	15192	11238	3715	159	11238	159	€0.45	€28,204
ab8	145	859	1023	11238	3715	1023	3715	€3.29	€71,452
ab10	3256	1103	45	1023	11238	45	11238	€2.25	€62,883

And the bottom:

hh14	20974	15192	11238	5211	45	11238	45	€0.45	€28,774
hh18	145	859	1023	11238	5211	1023	5211	€3.29	€81,296
hh110	3256	1103	45	1023	11238	45	11238	€2.25	€62,883
hh111	6523	298	5211	45	1023	5211	1023	€1.35	€26,101
Total Value									**€221,461**

1   08/12/2014

Stage 2

1. Select **Print** and **Preview** your layout, change the **Scaling** to **No Scaling**.

2. We are going to force page break so that certain products would definitely appear on the second page. From the **Page Layout** menu, insert a Page Break, so that the product codes eff4 onwards appear on the second page.

3. Return to **Print** and **Preview** your layout. You can see that the current layout will print on four pages.

4. Change the **Scaling** to **Fit all Columns on one Page**. The current layout will print on two pages.

5. Save your workbook.

The top of Page 2 in your Print, Preview should look as shown on the next page.

You should continue experimenting with the **Print**, **Settings** options, eg margins, to familiarise yourself further.

								Inventory	Valuation Widgets
eff4	20974	15192	11238	5211	45	11238	45	€0.45	€28,774
eff8	145	859	1023	11238	5211	1023	5211	€3.29	€81,296
eff10	3256	1103	45	1023	11238	45	11238	€2.25	€62,883
eff11	6523	298	5211	45	1023	5211	1023	€1.35	€26,101
eff10	3256	1103	45	5211	45	45	45	€2.25	€21,938
eff11	6523	298	5211	45	5211	5211	5211	€1.35	€37,409
g4	20974	15192	11238	5211	45	11238	45	€0.45	€28,774
g8	145	859	1023	11238	5211	1023	5211	€3.29	€81,296
g10	3256	1103	45	1023	11238	45	11238	€2.25	€62,883
g11	6523	298	5211	45	1023	5211	1023	€1.35	€26,101
hh14	20974	15192	11238	5211	45	11238	45	€0.45	€28,774
hh18	145	859	1023	11238	5211	1023	5211	€3.29	€81,296
hh110	3256	1103	45	1023	11238	45	11238	€2.25	€62,883
hh111	6523	298	5211	45	1023	5211	1023	€1.35	€26,101
Total Value									_€221,461_

You have now completed all the exercises for Chapter 4.

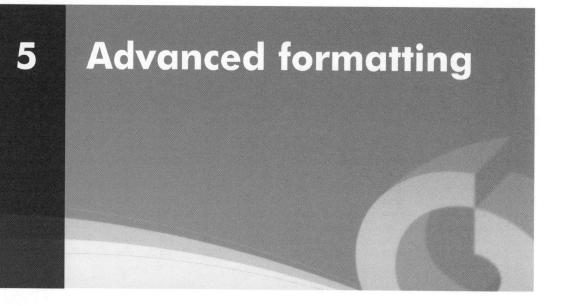

5 Advanced formatting

this chapter covers...

This chapter provides an introduction to advanced formatting for those new to spreadsheets.

The concepts and techniques covered are:

■ moving rows and columns

■ hiding rows and columns

■ cell display – borders, fill colours

■ alignments of data within a cell

■ conditional formatting

■ IF function

MOVING A COLUMN OR A ROW

Sometimes we may wish to change our basic layout and move either a column or a row within the layout.

For example, if we look at the expenditure forecast worksheet shown below:

	A	B	C	D	E	F	G	H
1	Expenditure forecast							
2								
3								
4		January	February	March	April	May	June	Average
5	Salaries	£80,000	£80,000	£80,000	£90,000	£90,000	£90,000	£85,000
6	Insurance	£1,000	£500	£0	£0	£0	£500	£333
7	Accountancy	£270	£0	£270	£0	£270	£0	£135
8	Advertising	£0	£1,500	£0	£0	£0	£1,800	£550
9	Postage	£95	£190	£95	£80	£95	£150	£118
10	Rent	£3,500	£3,500	£3,500	£3,500	£3,500	£3,500	£3,500
11	Stationery	£57	£90	£0	£90	£0	£90	£55
12	Totals	£84,922	£85,780	£83,865	£93,670	£93,865	£96,040	

We might wish to move the Average column to display before the months, to column B, as you can see in the image below:

	A	B	C	D	E	F	G	H
1	Expenditure forecast							
2								
3								
4		Average	January	February	March	April	May	June
5	Salaries	£85,000	£80,000	£80,000	£80,000	£90,000	£90,000	£90,000
6	Insurance	£333	£1,000	£500	£0	£0	£0	£500
7	Accountancy	£135	£270	£0	£270	£0	£270	£0
8	Advertising	£550	£0	£1,500	£0	£0	£0	£1,800
9	Postage	£118	£95	£190	£95	£80	£95	£150
10	Rent	£3,500	£3,500	£3,500	£3,500	£3,500	£3,500	£3,500
11	Stationery	£55	£57	£90	£0	£90	£0	£90
12	Totals		£84,922	£85,780	£83,865	£93,670	£93,865	£96,040

Alternatively, we might want to move the rows around so that the expenditure types are ordered alphabetically, as shown on the next page.

	A	B	C	D	E	F	G	H
1	Expenditure forecast							
2				Expenditure types now ordered alphabetically				
3								
4		Average	January	February	March	April	May	June
5	Accountancy	£135	£270	£0	£270	£0	£270	£0
6	Advertising	£550	£0	£1,500	£0	£0	£0	£1,800
7	Insurance	£333	£1,000	£500	£0	£0	£0	£500
8	Postage	£118	£95	£190	£95	£80	£95	£150
9	Rent	£3,500	£3,500	£3,500	£3,500	£3,500	£3,500	£3,500
10	Salaries	£85,000	£80,000	£80,000	£80,000	£90,000	£90,000	£90,000
11	Stationery	£55	£57	£90	£0	£90	£0	£90
12	Totals		£84,922	£85,780	£83,865	£93,670	£93,865	£96,040

To move a column:

■ right click on the column header of the column to move

■ select **Cut**

■ right click on the column header where you want to place the column

■ select **Insert cut cells**

or

■ insert a column in the position that you want to move the column to

■ click on the column header of the column to move

■ move the mouse over the edge of the column until you see the four headed arrow

■ click and drag the column to the blank column and release

To move a row:

■ right click on the row header of the row to move

■ select **Cut**

■ right click on the row header where you want to place the row

■ select **Insert cut cells**

or

■ insert a row in the position that you want to move the row to

■ click on the row header of the row to move

■ move the mouse over the edge of the row until you see the four headed arrow

■ click and drag the row to the blank row and release

HIDE A ROW OR A COLUMN

Sometimes we may wish to hide certain data or calculations used in a spreadsheet from public view, for example salary data.

The Hide row or column option allows us to do this and still make use of the data within our spreadsheet.

In the spreadsheet shown below, column B has been hidden.

	A	C	D	E	F	G	H	I
1	Expenditure forecast							
2		←		*Column B has been hidden*				
3								
4		January	February	March	April	May	June	
5	Accountancy	£270	£0	£270	£0	£270	£0	
6	Advertising	£0	£1,500	£0	£0	£0	£1,800	
7	Insurance	£1,000	£500	£0	£0	£0	£500	
8	Postage	£95	£190	£95	£80	£95	£150	
9	Rent	£3,500	£3,500	£3,500	£3,500	£3,500	£3,500	
10	Salaries	£80,000	£80,000	£80,000	£90,000	£90,000	£90,000	
11	Stationery	£57	£90	£0	£90	£0	£90	
12	Totals	£84,922	£85,780	£83,865	£93,670	£93,865	£96,040	

To hide a row:
- right click on the row header
- select **Hide**

To hide a column:
- right click on the column header
- select **Hide**

It is also possible to unhide a row or column to make modifications.

To unhide a row:
- select the row headers of the rows either side of the hidden row
- right click on the row headers
- select **Unhide**

To unhide a column:
- select the column headers of the columns either side of the hidden column
- right click on the column headers
- select **Unhide**

CELL DISPLAY

using borders

We sometimes want to make a cell or group of cells stand out within the spreadsheet.

One of the ways we can do this is to use Borders, which are just lines that we add around the edges of a cell or group of cells.

Borders can vary in colour and thickness; they can also be dotted or broken.

They can be used to split groups of numbers to improve legibility by applying the border to just one edge of a cell.

An example using borders is shown in the image below:

To apply borders:

- select all the required cells
- right click on the selected cell or cells
- select **Format cells**
- select **Border**
- choose the **Line style** and **Colour**
- apply to the required edges using either preset borders
- *or* select **Outline**, and click within the outline box to select edges (as shown in the screen illustration on the next page)

If you have more than one cell selected, **Outline** will put a border around the outer edge of the selected cells, and you can select to put borders between the cells horizontally or vertically by clicking within the outline.

To remove a border:

- select all the required cells
- right click on the selected cell or cells
- select **Format cells**
- select **Border**
- choose **None** from Presets

using font and fill colour

It is possible to change both the colour of the Font and the colour of the background within a cell, known as the Fill colour.

◢	A	B	C	D	E	F
1	Bank transactions					
2						
3	Opening balance	£1,500.00	←	*Cell fill color grey*		
4	Closing balance	£1,289.05		*with a thin border*		
5						
6	Date	Debit	Credit	Balance		
7	02/07/2014	£95.34	£0.00	£1,404.66		
8	11/07/2014	£0.00	£25.50	£1,430.16		
9	15/07/2014	£0.00	£34.78	£1,464.94		
10	22/07/2014	£67.90	£0.00	£1,397.04		
11	28/07/2014	£107.99	£0.00	£1,289.05		
12	Totals	£271.23	£60.28		£1,289.05	

To change the font colour:

- select all the required cells
- right click on the selected cell or cells
- select **Format cells**
- select **Font**
- choose the **Colour** you require

To set the cell Fill colour:

- select all the required cells
- right click on the selected cell or cells
- select **Format cells**
- select **Fill**
- choose the **Colour** you require

CELL ALIGNMENT

Alignment is used to describe the relative position of data within a cell.

With **left alignment** the data is shown up against the left edge of the cell.

Right alignment means that the data is shown up against the right edge of the cell.

For **centre alignment** the data is positioned in the centre of the cell.

Examples of all of these are shown in the screen below:

	A	B	C	D	E	F
1	Bank transactions					
2						
3	Opening balance	£1,500.00				
4	Closing balance	£1,289.05				
5						
6	Date	Debit	Credit	Balance		
7	02/07/2014	£95.34	£0.00	£1,404.66	◀━━━━	Left
8	11/07/2014	£0.00	£25.50	£1,430.16		
9	15/07/2014	£0.00	£34.78	£1,464.94	◀━━━━	Right
10	22/07/2014	£67.90	£0.00	£1,397.04		
11	28/07/2014	£107.99	£0.00	£1,289.05	◀━━━━	Centre
12	Totals	£271.23	£60.28		£1,289.05	

By default any text entered is aligned to the left. Data which is recognised as a number will be automatically aligned to the right.

To change the way data is aligned in a cell or cells:

- select the required cells, row or column
- right click on the selection
- select **Format cells**
- select the **Alignment** tab
- on the Horizontal dropdown select **Left**, **Right** or **Centre** as required

or with the cells selected

- click on the appropriate **Alignment** icon on the menu bar if visible

merged cells

Sometimes we have some text which we specifically want to spread across several cells, perhaps as a heading, and we may wish it to be centred across these cells.

To achieve this we effectively **merge** the cells together to make one big cell and then apply standard alignment options within this **merged cell**.

You can see in the example below that the merged cells (B6, C6, D6) are now treated as just one cell, when selected, and this allows us to centre the text over the three columns B, C and D within the merged cells.

	A	B	C	D	E	F	G
1	Bank transactions						
2							
3	Opening balance	£1,500.00					
4	Closing balance	£1,289.05					
5							
6			Transactions		*Merged and centred*		
7	Date	Debit	Credit	Balance			
8	02/07/2014	£95.34	£0.00	£1,404.66			
9	11/07/2014	£0.00	£25.50	£1,430.16			
10	15/07/2014	£0.00	£34.78	£1,464.94			
11	22/07/2014	£67.90	£0.00	£1,397.04			
12	28/07/2014	£107.99	£0.00	£1,289.05			
13	Totals	£271.23	£60.28		£1,289.05		

To merge cells:

- select the required cells
- right click on the selection
- select **Format cells**
- select the **Alignment** tab
- on the text control section click the **Merge cells** checkbox

or with the cells selected

■ click on the **Merge cells** icon on the menu bar if visible

word wrap

If the text which you enter into a cell is longer than the width of the cell, the text entered will appear as a single line of text across adjacent cells, as shown in the example below:

	C3		▾		*fx*	This is a piece of text to illustrate word wrap		
	A	B	C	D	E	F	G	H
1								
2								
3			This is a piece of text to illustrate word wrap					
4								
5								

If we want to force the text to fit in just column C, we can use word wrap, and the row height will automatically adjust to fit the text, without changing the column width, wrapping it into one cell.

This can be seen in the image below:

	C3		▾		*fx*	This is a piece of text to illustrate word wrap		
	A	B	C	D	E	F	G	H
1								
2		·						
3			This is a piece of text to illustrate word wrap					
4								

To apply word wrap to a cell:

■ select the required cells

either

■ select **Wrap Text** from the Home menu

or

■ right click on the selection

■ select **Format cells**

■ select the **Alignment** tab

■ on the text control section click the **Wrap text** checkbox

justify

If we have some text which has been word wrapped and occupies multiple lines within a cell, it is possible to **justify** the text, either horizontally or vertically.

The example below shows some text in a cell:

C3	▼	*fx*	This is a piece of text which has been wrapped

	A	B	C	D	E	F	G
1							
2							
3			This is a piece of text which has been wrapped and is now used to illustrate justify				
4							

If we now format the cell to justify horizontally, the text reformats as shown:

C3	▼	*fx*	This is a piece of text which has been wrapped

	A	B	C	D	E	F	G
1							
2							
3			This is a piece of text which has been wrapped and is now used to illustrate justify				
4							

The text has been spread horizontally, to fill the cell to the edges as much as possible.

To justify the contents of a cell:

- select the required cells
- right click on the selection
- select **Format cells**
- select the **Alignment** tab
- on the text alignment section

  for **Horizontal**, select **Justify** from the **Horizontal** drop-down list,

  or for **Vertical**, select **Justify** from the **Vertical** drop-down list

Note: Justification can be applied as a format to any cell, not just those containing text.

CONDITIONAL FORMATTING

We have covered the concepts of displaying cells with different fill colours and text colours, by selecting and changing.

Sometimes we may want a cell to change colour or display a different font automatically depending on the value it may hold; this is known as **conditional formatting**.

This is especially useful if we have a large amount of data, where it would be easy to miss seeing certain values.

Conditional formatting allows you to define a rule or rules, and if the data meets the rules (conditions), it will display in the format that you have specified, in a different font or fill colour.

For example, we may want all values less than £1,000 on a financial worksheet to be displayed in red text, so that they stand out.

Another example would be to display all negative (less than zero) values within a row or column in red.

logical operators

We can apply **comparison** 'operators' to create rules where **conditional formatting** can be used. These include:

- equal to
- greater than
- between
- less than
- text that contains
- a date occurring

Alternatively, we can create a **top/bottom** rule, these include:

- top 10 items
- top 10%
- bottom 10 items
- bottom 10%
- above average
- below average

You can define more than one rule, and each rule can have several conditions within it.

Once you have created a conditional formatting rule, you can edit the rule, to change the criteria, change cells you want to apply it to, or change the way the cells meeting the criteria are displayed.

In the example below we have created a conditional formatting rule to apply to the Postage costs in Cells B9 through to G9.

The rule is displayed below:

Show formatting rules for:	This Worksheet				
New Rule...	Edit Rule...	X Delete Rule	▲	▼	
Rule (applied in order shown)	Format		Applies to		Stop If True
Cell Value > 100	AaBbCcYyZz		=$B$9:$G$9		☐

Note $ symbols are automatically inserted within the cell range, the meaning of these $ symbols is described in detail in the next chapter.

As you can see in the image below, all cells where Postage costs are greater than £100 are shown filled with a grey background.

◢	A	B	C	D	E	F	G
1	Expenditure forecast						
2							
3		January	February	March	April	May	June
4	Salaries	£80,000	£80,000	£80,000	£90,000	£90,000	£90,000
5	Insurance	£1,000	£500	£0	£0	£0	£500
6	Rent	£3,500	£3,500	£3,500	£3,500	£3,500	£3,500
7	Accountancy	£270	£0	£270	£0	£270	£0
8	Advertising	£0	£1,500	£0	£0	£0	£1,800
9	Postage	£95	£190	£95	£80	£95	£150
10	Stationery	£57	£0	£0	£90	£0	£90
11	Totals	£84,922	£85,730	£83,865	£93,670	£93,865	£96,040
12							
13				*Values exceed £100*			

To set conditional formatting for a group of cells:

- select the required cells
- select **Conditional formatting** from the menu bar
- enter the rule which you want to apply using the drop-down list of 'greater than, less than, equal to' etc, and the required value
- select the **Font style** and **Colour**, together with the **Fill** colour and any other effects

  either from choices in the drop-down list,

  or by selecting **Custom format** from the bottom of the list, and choosing from the standard format cells options.

To clear conditional formatting for a group of cells:

■ select the required cells

■ select **Conditional formatting**

■ select **Clear Rules**, then **Clear rules from selected cells**

To clear all conditional formatting for a worksheet:

■ select **Conditional formatting**

■ select **Clear Rules**, then **Clear rules from entire sheet**

LOGICAL FUNCTIONS AND OPERATORS

A concept used regularly in spreadsheets is **conditional logic**.

This is a concept where if something is true, then something else happens.

For example:

> **if** *I swim in the sea* **then** *I will get wet*
>
> **if** *I do no work* **then** *I will not pass my exams*

Within the spreadsheet environment, we often want to test a cell for a certain value, and

■ if it is this value we make one thing happen

■ if it is not this value, we want something different to happen

logical operators

We can apply the standard comparison 'operators' to create situations where **conditional logic** can be used. These include:

■ equal to (=)

■ greater than (>)

■ greater than or equal to (>=)

■ less than (<)

■ less than or equal to(<=)

■ not equal to (<>)

For example, a condition could be that cell B10 is greater than 100 which we would express as:

IF B10>100 then …

The main logical function which is used in spreadsheets is the **IF( )** function.

IF

The **IF** function returns one value if the condition you specify evaluates to TRUE, and another value if that condition evaluates to FALSE.

For example, if you take an exam and the pass mark is 55%, if you get 60% you will pass, and if you get 54% you will fail.

Using the IF function you can use a spreadsheet to work out the 'pass' or 'fail' for you, as we will see in the example on the next page.

The IF function is made up of three parts:

=IF(logical test,value if true,value if false)

These three parts can be explained as follows:

■ **logical test**

This can be any value or expression which can be evaluated to TRUE or FALSE. In the case of the exam pass mark this is =IF(F4>=55% . . .) the logical test here is whether the mark in cell F4 is greater than or equal to 55%.

■ **value if true**

This is the value which will be returned by the function if the condition evaluates to TRUE. If the value is 60% the answer is "PASS".

■ **value if false**

This is the value which will be returned by the function if the condition evaluates to FALSE. If the value is 54% or less (ie less than the pass mark of 55%) the answer is "FAIL".

Therefore, to recap, the structure of the IF function is as follows:

=IF(logical test,value if true,value if false)

In the example we used to work out exam success or failure on the basis of a 55% pass mark, the IF function will be expressed as follows:

=IF(F4>=55%,"PASS","FAIL")

Note that:

■ any text which is to appear in the spreadsheet should be shown in quotes: **"PASS"**

■ the third part of the function (ie 'value if false') is optional; if it is not included, no value will be returned if the condition is false

In the example screen on the next page, we have entered formulas in column G, for each person.

The formula in cell G4 for John Smith is:

=IF(F4>=55%,"PASS","FAIL")

This formula looks at the value in cell F4, and since it more than 55%, this returns a value of PASS in cell G4.

Similarly for Harpret Bhopal, the formula in cell G5 is:

=IF(F5>=55%,"PASS","FAIL")

This formula returns a value of FAIL because Harpret Bhopal's average is less than 55%.

G4				f_x	=IF(F4>=55%,"PASS","FAIL")	
	A	B	C	D	E	F	G
1	**Midterm exams**						
2							
3	**Name**	**Module1**	**Module2**	**Module3**	**Module4**	**Average**	
4	*John Smith*	75%	62%	45%	65%	61.75%	PASS
5	*Harpret Bhopal*	61%	48%			54.50%	FAIL
6	*Wendy Owen*	63%	80%	51%	41%	58.75%	PASS
7	*Mohammed Iqbal*	53%		41%	64%	52.67%	FAIL
8	*Barbara White*	42%	63%	85%	43%	58.25%	PASS

Note: If we wanted to either specify PASS or leave it blank, a blank is "" (empty quote marks), so our formula would be:

=IF(F5>=55%,"PASS","")

Let's look at another example.

Suppose we had a costing sheet containing **Budget** figures for our expected costs (column B) and **Actual** figures for each of these costs (column C). In column D we have calculated the **Variance** (Budget – Actual), as shown in the image below:

	A	B	C	D	E	F
1	**Costing comparison**					
2						
3	**Cost Type**	**Budget**	**Actual**	**Variance**	**Adverse**	**Favourable**
4	Direct Materials	£12,000	£18,500	-£6,500		
5	Direct Labour	£25,000	£24,500	£500		
6	Production Overheads	£15,000	£18,900	-£3,900		
7	Administration Overheads	£6,500	£5,050	£1,450		
8	Selling & Distribution Overheads	£11,000	£12,000	-£1,000		

We could manually identify whether the Actual figure compared to the Budget figure is Adverse (greater than Budget) or Favourable (less than Budget), but we are going to use the IF function to do it for us.

In cell E4, we are going to put the formula: IF(D4<0, D4,0)

This formula equates to: if the value in D4 is less than zero, ie the variance is less than 0, put the value of D4 in cell E4, otherwise, put 0 in E4.

The results are shown in the image below:

E4		f_x	=IF(D4<0,D4,0)			
	A	B	C	D	E	F
1	Costing comparison					
2						
3	Cost Type	Budget	Actual	Variance	Adverse	Favourable
4	Direct Materials	£12,000	£18,500	-£6,500	-£6,500	
5	Direct Labour	£25,000	£24,500	£500	£0	
6	Production Overheads	£15,000	£18,900	-£3,900	-£3,900	
7	Administration Overheads	£6,500	£5,050	£1,450	£0	
8	Selling & Distribution Overheads	£11,000	£12,000	-£1,000	-£1,000	

Similarly, in the Favourable column, F4 we put the formula:

=IF(D4>0, D4,0)

This formula equates to: if the value in D4 is greater than zero, ie the variance is greater than 0, put the value of D4 in cell F4, otherwise, put 0 in F4.

Again, this can be seen below:

F4		f_x	=IF(D4>0,D4,0)			
	A	B	C	D	E	F
1	Costing comparison					
2						
3	Cost Type	Budget	Actual	Variance	Adverse	Favourable
4	Direct Materials	£12,000	£18,500	-£6,500	-£6,500	£0
5	Direct Labour	£25,000	£24,500	£500	£0	£500
6	Production Overheads	£15,000	£18,900	-£3,900	-£3,900	£0
7	Administration Overheads	£6,500	£5,050	£1,450	£0	£1,450
8	Selling & Distribution Overheads	£11,000	£12,000	-£1,000	-£1,000	£0

Chapter Summary

This chapter has covered in detail the following topics:

■ moving rows and columns

■ hiding rows and columns

■ cell display – borders, fill colours

■ alignments of data within a cell

■ conditional formatting

■ IF function

You should now carry out some or all of the exercises on the next few pages in order to practise and reinforce your learning.

Activities

Exercise 1 – formatting and presentation

In this first exercise we are going to create a template for an invoice. We will start with an invoice similar to that which we created in Chapter 3.

Stage 1

In this stage we start to create the basic empty layout of our invoice:

1. Download the file **Ch5Invoice** from www.osbornebooks.co.uk.

2. Save this workbook with the name **Ch5Exercise1**.

The workbook should look as shown below:

	A	B	C	D	E	F	G	H
1	Invoice Date:	01/12/2014						
2								
3	Customer No.:	1498						
4								
5	Product	Description	Qty	Price	Unit	Total	Discount	Net
6	Code			£		£	%	£
7	PAPER-R	Paper -Ream	4	2.15	each	8.60	5%	8.17
8	PEN-50	Pens box - 50	2	9.99	each	19.98	10%	17.98
9	A4FOLD-3	A4 Ring Folder - 3	3	2.50	each	7.50	5%	7.13
10	PAD-1	Lined pads - 1	6	1.70	each	10.20	2%	10.00
11	ENVA4-100	Envelopes A4 -100	3	10.99	each	32.97	4%	31.65
12							Subtotal	74.92
13							VAT (20%)	14.98
14							TOTAL	89.91

3. Insert a column to the left of column A.

4. Insert two rows before row 1.

5. Merge cells C1 through to F1, enter the text My Company Ltd, centred and font size 16.

6. Remove the underline from Invoice Date (B3), and Customer No (B5).

7. Widen column B to 15.

8. Clear the Invoice Date, and Customer No from cells C3 and C5.

9. In Cell E3, enter **Invoice No.:** and widen column E to 12.

10. Widen column F to 12.

11. Save your workbook as **Ch5Exercise1**.

Your worksheet should look as shown in the image below.

⊿	A	B	C	D	E	F	G	H	I
1			My Company Ltd						
2									
3		Invoice Date:			Invoice No.:				
4									
5		Customer No.:							
6									
7		Product	Description	Qty	Price	Unit	Total	Discount	Net
8		Code			£		£	%	£
9		PAPER-R	Paper -Ream	4	2.15	each	8.60	5%	8.17
10		PEN-50	Pens box - 50	2	9.99	each	19.98	10%	17.98
11		A4FOLD-3	A4 Ring Folder - 3	3	2.50	each	7.50	5%	7.13
12		PAD-1	Lined pads - 1	6	1.70	each	10.20	2%	10.00
13		ENVA4-100	Envelopes A4 -100	3	10.99	each	32.97	4%	31.65
14								Subtotal	74.92
15								VAT (20%)	14.98
16								TOTAL	89.91

Stage 2

In this section we are going to introduce borders, and fill some of the cells to make data entry clearer:

1. Format cells B3, C3, B5, C5, E3 and F3 so that they have a thin solid black border all the way round.

2. Cells C3, C5 and F3 should be filled with a light grey.

3. Clear cells B9 through to F13 (Product Code through to Unit).

Note: we have formulas in columns G, H and I so do not clear these cells.

4. Clear cells H9 to H13 (Discount %).

5. Insert 3 blank rows between rows 10 and 11.

6. Copy row 10 into each of these blank rows (this will ensure all the formulas are copied into the new rows.

7. Save your workbook.

The workbook is shown in the image at the top of the next page:

▲	A	B	C	D	E	F	G	H	I
1					My Company Ltd				
2									
3		Invoice Date:			Invoice No.:				
4									
5		Customer No.:							
6									
7		Product	Description	Qty	Price	Unit	Total	Discount	Net
8		Code			£		£	%	£
9							0.00		0.00
10							0.00		0.00
11							0.00		0.00
12							0.00		0.00
13							0.00		0.00
14							0.00		0.00
15							0.00		0.00
16							0.00		0.00
17								Subtotal	0.00
18								VAT (20%)	0.00
19								TOTAL	0.00
20									

Stage 3

We are now going to format the detail part of the invoice.

1. Apply thin solid black borders to cells B7 through to I8 to produce format as shown below:

Product	Description	Qty	Price	Unit	Total	Discount	Net
Code			£		£	%	£

2. Apply thin solid black borders to cells B9 through to I16 to produce format as shown below:

Product	Description	Qty	Price	Unit	Total	Discount	Net
Code			£		£	%	£
					0.00		0.00
					0.00		0.00
					0.00		0.00
					0.00		0.00
					0.00		0.00
					0.00		0.00
					0.00		0.00
					0.00		0.00

3. Apply alignment **word wrap** to cells C9 to C16 (the description column) this is to allow for descriptions which may be longer than the width of the column.

4. Align the headings for each of the columns to centre (rows 7 and 8).

5. Rename the worksheet as Template.

6. You have now completed your template, save your workbook.

Your template should look as follows:

	A	B	C	D	E	F	G	H	I
1			My Company Ltd						
2									
3		Invoice Date:			Invoice No.:				
4									
5		Customer No.:							
6									
7		Product	Description	Qty	Price	Unit	Total	Discount	Net
8		Code			£		£	%	£
9							0.00		0.00
10							0.00		0.00
11							0.00		0.00
12							0.00		0.00
13							0.00		0.00
14							0.00		0.00
15							0.00		0.00
16							0.00		0.00
17								Subtotal	0.00
18								VAT (20%)	0.00
19								TOTAL	0.00

Stage 4

We are now going to enter one simple invoice into our template:

1. Enter Invoice details as follows:

Invoice Date: 20/11/14

Invoice No.: 15911

Customer No.: 63412

Product code: SCREWS-20

Description: 20ml screw with tungsten tip, contains 25

Qty: 5

Price: £5.99

Unit: each

Discount: 5%

Product code: WASHERS-20

Description: 20ml brass washers, contains 50

Qty: 5

Price: £3.99

Unit: each

Discount: 5%

2. Save your workbook as **Ch5ExerciseInv**.

3. Print your invoice, landscape or fit to one page and portrait, the printout should be as shown below:

My Company Ltd

Invoice Date:	20/11/2014		Invoice No.:	15911

Customer No.:	63412

Product Code	Description	Qty	Price £	Unit	Total £	Discount %	Net £
SCREWS-20	20ml screw with tungsten tip contains 25	5	5.99	each	29.95	5%	28.45
WASHERS-20	20ml brass washers contains 50	5	3.99	each	19.95	5%	18.95
					0.00		0.00
					0.00		0.00
					0.00		0.00
					0.00		0.00
					0.00		0.00
					0.00		0.00
						Subtotal	47.41
						VAT (20%)	9.48
						TOTAL	56.89

Exercise 2 – conditional formatting

In this second exercise we are going to make use of conditional formatting in an inventory situation, to help us identify when inventory of a product is low.

Stage 1

In this stage we are going to work with an inventory list which has already been created.

1. Download the file **Ch5InventoryList**.

2. Save this workbook with the name **Ch5Exercise2**.

The workbook should look as shown below:

	A	B	C	D	E	F
1	Inventory report					
2						
3	Product code	Inventory	Price	Value	Re-order Level	
4	ab1	967	£2.50	£2,416	174	
5	ab2	946	£3.25	£3,074	286	
6	ab3	458	£0.99	£453	677	
7	ab4	149	£0.45	£67	32	
8	ab8	73	£3.29	£241	454	
9	ab10	663	£2.25	£1,492	177	
10	ab11	890	£1.35	£1,201	790	
11	bb4	7	£0.45	£3	961	
12	bb8	825	£3.29	£2,715	650	

The **Re-order Level** column tells us the inventory of each item we like to hold. If the **Inventory** figure has fallen below this number, then we need to re-order.

In column F we are going to compare the Inventory figure, with the Re-order Level.

3.   In cell F3, enter the text **Inventory v Re-order**, set the cell format to word wrap.

4.   In cell E4, enter the formula for **Inventory** minus **Re-order Level** (B4-E4)

5.   Copy the formula for each of the products.

6.   Apply conditional formatting (**Highlight cell rules**), to column F, so that all cells where the number is negative (less than 0) are displayed with a custom format, black text and a dark grey fill.

7.   Save your workbook.

The image on the next page shows the results.

	A	B	C	D	E	F
1	Inventory report					
2						
3	Product code	Inventory	Price	Value	Re-order Level	Inventory v Re-order
4	ab1	967	£2.50	£2,416	174	793
5	ab2	946	£3.25	£3,074	286	660
6	ab3	458	£0.99	£453	677	-219
7	ab4	149	£0.45	£67	32	117
8	ab8	73	£3.29	£241	454	-381
9	ab10	663	£2.25	£1,492	177	486
10	ab11	890	£1.35	£1,201	790	100
11	bb4	7	£0.45	£3	961	-954

Stage 2

In this stage we are going to experiment with some other conditional formatting.

We want to look at the values of inventory which we are holding.

1. In the Value column (column D), using conditional formatting, highlight the top 10 inventory values, display with a custom format, black border and no fill.

The results are shown below:

	A	B	C	D	E	F
1	Inventory report					
2						
3	Product code	Inventory	Price	Value	Re-order Level	Inventory v Re-order
4	ab1	967	£2.50	£2,416	174	793
5	ab2	946	£3.25	£3,074	286	660
6	ab3	458	£0.99	£453	677	-219
7	ab4	149	£0.45	£67	32	117
8	ab8	73	£3.29	£241	454	-381
9	ab10	663	£2.25	£1,492	177	486
10	ab11	890	£1.35	£1,201	790	100
11	bb4	7	£0.45	£3	961	-954
12	bb8	825	£3.29	£2,715	650	176

We now want to identify our 10 lowest priced items.

2. In the Price column (column C), using conditional formatting, highlight the lowest 10 priced item values, display with a custom format, italic font, and a light grey fill.

3. Save your workbook.

The results are shown below:

	A	B	C	D	E	F
1	Inventory report					
2						
3	Product code	Inventory	Price	Value	Re-order Level	Inventory v Re-order
4	ab1	967	£2.50	£2,416	174	793
5	ab2	946	£3.25	£3,074	286	660
6	ab3	458	*£0.99*	£453	677	-219
7	ab4	149	*£0.45*	£67	32	117
8	ab8	73	£3.29	£241	454	-381
9	ab10	663	£2.25	£1,492	177	486
10	ab11	890	£1.35	£1,201	790	100
11	bb4	7	*£0.45*	£3	961	-954
12	bb8	825	£3.29	£2,715	650	176

Exercise 3 – using the IF function

In this third exercise using the same workbook, we are going make use of the IF function to help us identify when inventory of a product is low.

Stage 1

In this stage we are going to work with an inventory list which has already been created:

1. Re-open the file **Ch5Exercise2**.

2. Save this workbook with the name **Ch5Exercise3**.

3. Clear all conditional formatting rules from the worksheet.

4. Remove the formulas from column F.

5. In cell F3, enter the text **Re-order?**

6. Widen column F so that the text fits all on one row.

7. In cell F4, enter the formula to compare the value in cell B4, with the value in E4, and if B4 is less (ie less than the re-order level), than put the YES in cell F4, otherwise leave it blank.

8. Copy this formula in column F for the other products.

9. Format column F, so that the text is right aligned.

10. Save your workbook.

Your workbook should look as shown below:

F4			f_x	=IF(B4<E4,"YES","")		
	A	B	C	D	E	F
1	Inventory report					
2						
3	Product code	Inventory	Price	Value	Re-order Level	Re-order?
4	ab1	967	£2.50	£2,416	174	
5	ab2	946	£3.25	£3,074	286	
6	ab3	458	£0.99	£453	677	YES
7	ab4	149	£0.45	£67	32	
8	ab8	73	£3.29	£241	454	YES
9	ab10	663	£2.25	£1,492	177	
10	ab11	890	£1.35	£1,201	790	
11	bb4	7	£0.45	£3	961	YES
12	bb8	825	£3.29	£2,715	650	

Stage 2

In this stage we are going to calculate new prices for each inventory item, based on the existing price

1. In cell G3, enter text **New Price**, **word wrap** the text.

2. Format column G to be **currency £**, with **two decimal places**.

    For all prices which are more than £1 we are going to increase by £0.50, and for those less than £1 we are going to increase by £0.25.

3. Enter a formula in cell G4, such that, if the value in C4 is > 1 then put the value of C4+0.5 in G4, otherwise enter the value of C4+0.25 .

4. Copy the formula to the other product rows.

5. Move the New Price column, to between the Price and Value columns (column C and column D).

6. Save your workbook.

Your workbook should look as shown below:

D4			f_x	=IF(C4>1,C4+0.5,C4+0.25)		
A	**B**	**C**	**D**	**E**	**F**	**G**
1 Inventory report						
2						
3 Product code	Inventory	Price	New Price	Value	Re-order Level	Re-order?
4 ab1	967	£2.50	£3.00	£2,416	174	
5 ab2	946	£3.25	£3.75	£3,074	286	
6 ab3	458	£0.99	£1.24	£453	677	YES
7 ab4	149	£0.45	£0.70	£67	32	
8 ab8	73	£3.29	£3.79	£241	454	YES
9 ab10	663	£2.25	£2.75	£1,492	177	
10 ab11	890	£1.35	£1.85	£1,201	790	
11 bb4	7	£0.45	£0.70	£3	961	YES
12 bb8	825	£3.29	£3.79	£2,715	650	
13 bb10	236	£2.25	£2.75	£530	31	
14 bb11	562	£1.35	£1.85	£758	782	YES
15 cb4	456	£0.45	£0.70	£205	289	
16 cb8	537	£3.29	£3.79	£1,767	111	

Stage 3

In this final stage we are going to identify products where we have a high inventory balance compared to the re-order level.

1. In cell H3, enter text **High Inventory**, **word wrap** the text.

We want to identify all products where the **Inventory** is more than **three** times the **re-order level**.

2. In H4, create an **IF** formula which puts **YES** in H4, if B4/F4 >3, or leaves it **blank** if this is false.

3. Copy the formula to the other product rows.

4. Align all of column H to the **right**.

5. Save your workbook.

Your workbook should look as shown below:

H4			f_x	=IF(B4/F4>3,"YES","")			
	A	B	C	D	E	F	G	H
1	Inventory report							
2								
3	Product code	Inventory	Price	New Price	Value	Re-order Level	Re-order?	High Inventory
4	ab1	967	£2.50	£3.00	£2,416	174		YES
5	ab2	946	£3.25	£3.75	£3,074	286		YES
6	ab3	458	£0.99	£1.24	£453	677	YES	
7	ab4	149	£0.45	£0.70	£67	32		YES
8	ab8	73	£3.29	£3.79	£241	454	YES	
9	ab10	663	£2.25	£2.75	£1,492	177		YES
10	ab11	890	£1.35	£1.85	£1,201	790		
11	bb4	7	£0.45	£0.70	£3	961	YES	
12	bb8	825	£3.29	£3.79	£2,715	650		
13	bb10	236	£2.25	£2.75	£530	31		YES
14	bb11	562	£1.35	£1.85	£758	782	YES	
15	cb4	456	£0.45	£0.70	£205	289		
16	cb8	537	£3.29	£3.79	£1,767	111		YES

6 Advanced formulas and formula validation

this chapter covers...

This chapter covers more on formulas including checking for errors and different ways of referencing cells.

The concepts and techniques covered are:

- *cell addressing*
- *formulas – errors*
- *working with multiple worksheets*
- *working with multiple workbooks*

CELL ADDRESSING

The way in which a cell is referenced is known as its address, for example A12, B49. This becomes important when we are using formulas. We have two ways of referencing cells within formulas:

■ relative addressing

■ absolute addressing

relative addressing

As we have seen, when we copy a formula from one cell to another, the formula is automatically adjusted to reflect the row or column of the new cell. This is called relative addressing: the formula is adjusted relative to the new cell.

We have seen that if you copy the formula

=SUM(B3:E3)

down a row from cell F3 to cell F4, the formula becomes

=SUM(B4:E4)

Similarly, for columns if you copy the formula

=SUM(B4:B8)

from cell B9 across a column to cell C9, the formula becomes

= SUM(C4:C8)

absolute addressing

Sometimes we do not want the cell reference to change as we copy a formula – we want to keep a reference to an original cell or cells. To do this we use the dollar sign: $.

For example, $C$3 would refer to cell C3, and, when placed in a formula and copied, the copies would all also retain this reference to C3.

In the example below we have entered an hourly rate in cell C3, which we wish to apply to all the weekly hrs totals (row 11). We have created a formula in cell C13 to give us a monetary value for the work carried out the week 1st Apr using the formula:

=C11*C3

	SUM	▼	✗ ✓ *fx*	=C11*C3			

◢	A	B	C	D	E	F	G	H
1			Hours worked					
2								
3		Hourly Rate	£7.50					
4								
5		Week Beg	1st Apr	8th Apr	15th Apr	22nd Apr	29th Apr	
6		Mon	7	8.5	7	8	6.5	
7		Tue	6.5	6.5	7	7.5	7.5	
8		Wed	5.5	7.5	7	6	8	
9		Thu	6.5	6.5	6.5	7.5	7	
10		Fri	7.5	7.5	7.5	5	7.5	
11		Weekly hrs:	33	36.5	35	34	36.5	
12								
13		Weekly pay:	=C11*C3					
14								

You can see the two cells used in the formula highlighted.

We will now change the formula to =C11*$C$3 so that we can copy it and still keep the reference to C3, the cell where the hourly rate of £7.50 is entered.

	SUM	▼	✗ ✓ *fx*	=C11*$C$3			

◢	A	B	C	D	E	F	G
1			Hours worked				
2							
3		Hourly Rate	£7.50				
4							
5		Week Beg	1st Apr	8th Apr	15th Apr	22nd Apr	29th Apr
6		Mon	7	8.5	7	8	6.5
7		Tue	6.5	6.5	7	7.5	7.5
8		Wed	5.5	7.5	7	6	8
9		Thu	6.5	6.5	6.5	7.5	7
10		Fri	7.5	7.5	7.5	5	7.5
11		Weekly hrs:	33	36.5	35	34	36.5
12							
13		Weekly pay:	=C11*$C$3				
14							

When the formula =C11*$C$3 is then copied to cell D13 through to G13, you can see the formula in cell G13 keeps the reference to C3, as shown in the image on the next page.

SUM	▾	●	✕ ✓ ƒx	=G11*$C$3		

◢	A	B	C	D	E	F	G
1			Hours worked				
2							
3		Hourly Rate	£7.50				
4							
5		**Week Beg**	**1st Apr**	**8th Apr**	**15th Apr**	**22nd Apr**	**29th Apr**
6		Mon	7	8.5	7	8	6.5
7		Tue	6.5	6.5	7	7.5	7.5
8		Wed	5.5	7.5	7	6	8
9		Thu	6.5	6.5	6.5	7.5	7
10		Fri	7.5	7.5	7.5	5	7.5
11		Weekly hrs:	33	36.5	35	34	36.5
12							
13		Weekly pay:	£247.50	£273.75	£262.50	£255.00	=G11*$C$3

If the hourly rate changes from £7.50 to £8, then all you need to do is amend the amount entered in cell C3, and all the weekly pay values are re-calculated, as shown in the image below:

C3	▾	●		ƒx	8	

◢	A	B	C	D	E	F	G
1			Hours worked				
2							
3		Hourly Rate	£8.00				
4							
5		**Week Beg**	**1st Apr**	**8th Apr**	**15th Apr**	**22nd Apr**	**29th Apr**
6		Mon	7	8.5	7	8	6.5
7		Tue	6.5	6.5	7	7.5	7.5
8		Wed	5.5	7.5	7	6	8
9		Thu	6.5	6.5	6.5	7.5	7
10		Fri	7.5	7.5	7.5	5	7.5
11		Weekly hrs:	33	36.5	35	34	36.5
12							
13		Weekly pay:	£264.00	£292.00	£280.00	£272.00	£292.00

Absolute cell addressing is a very important part of creating formulas within spreadsheets.

It is especially useful if you want to use one value such as a rate, within lots of calculations, this removes the need for duplicating the value in many places and reduces errors.

FORMULA VALIDATION

We have explained formulas and how to create them earlier in this book. We are now going to explain some of the ways of checking that the formulas we have entered are doing what we expect them to do. The methods which we are going to cover are:

- show formulas
- error checking
- circular references
- trace precedents
- trace dependents

show formulas

This is a simple visual method, where formulas are displayed within the sheet. The example below shows the worksheet displayed in the normal way:

⊿	A	B	C	D	E	F	G
1		Hours worked					
2							
3		Hourly Rate	£8.00			Date	05/05/2014
4							
5		**Week Beg**	**1st Apr**	**8th Apr**	**15th Apr**	**22nd Apr**	**29th Apr**
6		Mon	7	8.5	7	8	6.5
7		Tue	6.5	6.5	7	7.5	7.5
8		Wed	5.5	7.5	7	6	8
9		Thu	6.5	6.5	6.5	7.5	7
10		Fri	7.5	7.5	7.5	5	7.5
11		Weekly hrs:	33	36.5	35	34	36.5
12							
13		Weekly pay:	£264.00	£292.00	£280.00	£272.00	£292.00

We then select **Show Formulas** from the Formulas tab and the way in which the cells display changes, as shown on the next page:

◢ A	B	C	D	E	F	G
1			Hours worked			
2						
3	Hourly Rate	8			Date	41764
4						
5	**Week Beg**	**1st Apr**	**8th Apr**	**15th Apr**	**22nd Apr**	**29th Apr**
6	Mon	7	8.5	7	8	6.5
7	Tue	6.5	6.5	7	7.5	7.5
8	Wed	5.5	7.5	7	6	8
9	Thu	6.5	6.5	6.5	7.5	7
10	Fri	7.5	7.5	7.5	5	7.5
11	Weekly hrs:	=SUM(C6:C10)	=SUM(D6:D10)	=SUM(E6:E10)	=SUM(F6:F10)	=SUM(G6:G10)
12						
13	Weekly pay:	=C11*$C$3	=D11*$C$3	=E11*$C$3	=F11*$C$3	=G11*$C$3

In the screen above we can see the actual data or formulas contained in each cell without any formatting.

Rows 11 and 13 show the mathematical formulas we entered to total the hours and calculate the weekly pay.

In cell G3 where we have a date, what we now see is the serial number representation of the date. Dates are stored as serial numbers so that they can be used in calculations. The number represents the number of days since 0-Jan-1900, ie 1-jan-1900 is shown as 1. You can see our date of 05/05/2014 is shown as 41764.

In a relatively small worksheet, or a particular section of a larger worksheet, it is possible to check that the formulas that have been entered are correct by using the **Show Formulas** option.

The worksheet can be printed in this form using the normal print options.

To revert to the normal display we select **Show Formulas** again from the menu bar and select the appropriate command.

As mentioned, this is a fairly basic way of checking formulas. There is a more automated way using a facility called **error checking**, which is available in most spreadsheet packages.

error checking

The **error checking** facility checks for common errors which occur in formulas. These include:

■ formulas that result in an error, such as dividing by zero

■ numbers formatted as text, or preceded by an apostrophe (')

■ formulas inconsistent with other formulas near them

■ formulas which omit cells which are near others which have been included in the formula (eg a range of cells)

■ cells containing circular references

Any cells where the formula contains an error are flagged with a small green triangle in the upper-left corner of the cell.

In the same way that we can have our word processing package checking for errors as we type, it is possible to set the spreadsheet package options, so that our formulas are checked as we enter them; this is known as **automatic error checking**. Alternatively we can use the **error checking facility** at any time to check through the whole worksheet.

If we take the Hours worked spreadsheet shown on the previous page we can modify the formula in cell F11:

from **=SUM(F6:F10)**

to **=SUM(F6:F9)**

You can see in the image below, that when we have automatic checking on, we get a small triangle in the upper left of cell F11, indicating a formula error or warning.

A	B	C	D	E	F	G
1		Hours worked				
2						
3	Hourly Rate	£8.00			Date	05/05/2014
4						
5	Week Beg	1st Apr	8th Apr	15th Apr	22nd Apr	29th Apr
6	Mon	7	8.5	7	8	6.5
7	Tue	6.5	6.5	7	7.5	7.5
8	Wed	5.5	7.5	7	6	8
9	Thu	6.5	6.5	6.5	7.5	7
10	Fri	7.5	7.5	7.5	5	7.5
11	Weekly hrs:	33	36.5	35	29	36.5
12						
13	Weekly pay:	£264.00	£292.00	£280.00	£232.00	£292.00

If we then select cell F11 we get an exclamation icon and a description of the error – 'Inconsistent Formula' – which tells us that this formula does not match the pattern of the formulas above and below (or to either side in the same row.) Here cell F11 is inconsistent with the other formulas in Row F.

F11			f_x	=SUM(F6:F9)	

	A	B	C	D	E	F	G
4							
5		**Week Beg**	**1st Apr**	**8th Apr**	**15th Apr**	**22nd Apr**	**29th Apr**
6		Mon	7	8.5	7	8	6.5
7		Tue	6.5	6.5	7	7.5	7.5
8		Wed	5.5	7.5	7	6	8
9		Thu	6.5	6.5	6.5	7.5	7
10		Fri	7.5	7.5	7.5	5	7.5
11		Weekly hrs:	33	36.5	⚠ ▾	29	36.5
12							
13		Weekly pay:	£264.00	£292.00	£2		
14							
15							
16							
17							

Inconsistent Formula

Copy Formula from <u>L</u>eft

<u>H</u>elp on this error

<u>I</u>gnore Error

Edit in <u>F</u>ormula Bar

Error Checking <u>O</u>ptions...

◄◄ ◄ ► ►◄   Time data / Sheet2 / Sheet3 / ☺

Ready

To set your choices for error checking:

■ select **Options** from the appropriate menu

■ select **Formulas**

■ either check or uncheck **Enable Background error checking** as required

■ check or uncheck the **Rules** to configure as you require

Note that if the formula is actually what we want we can instruct the error check to **ignore the error**.

To perform a full worksheet error check:

■ select **Error check** (or its equivalent) from the menu

The rules will be applied as set up in the Options described above, and any cells with a formula error will be flagged as described on the previous page.

circular references

This error occurs when a cell's formula contains a reference to itself, for example if cell F11 contained the formula:

=SUM(F6:F11)

we would get an error warning, as shown below:

Circular Reference Warning

One or more formulas contain a circular reference and may not calculate correctly. Circular references are any references within a formula that depend upon the results of that same formula. For example, a cell that refers to its own value or a cell that refers to another cell which depends on the original cell's value both contain circular references.

For more information about understanding, finding, and removing circular references, click Help. If you want to create a circular reference, click OK to continue.

[OK]   [Help]

If we select Ok, the formula will be left in the cell, but is unlikely to produce the result we require. The small triangle will display in the upper left of cell F11, indicating a formula warning.

The **Error Checking** menu displays a drop-down list of options. One of the items in the list is **Circular References**. Clicking this item will cause a list of those cells containing circular references to be displayed. If you click on any of the cells in the list, the cursor will move to that cell and you can edit the formula. When all circular references have been resolved, the list will be empty.

trace precedents

The **Trace Precedents** facility allows you to identify those cells which **affect** the value of the currently selected cell.

For example if cell D4 contained the formula

=A3 +B3

both A3 and B3 would be **precedents** of D4, since they both affect the value of D4.

If we take our Hours worked spreadsheet as an example, and select cell F13, which holds the formula

=F11*$C$3

as illustrated in the show formulas screen below:

	F13	▼	⊙	fx	=F11*$C$3	
	A	B	C	D	E	F	G
1				Hours worked			
2							
3		Hourly Rate	8			Date	41764
4							
5		**Week Beg**	**1st Apr**	**8th Apr**	**15th Apr**	**22nd Apr**	**29th Apr**
6		Mon	7	8.5	7	8	6.5
7		Tue	6.5	6.5	7	7.5	7.5
8		Wed	5.5	7.5	7	6	8
9		Thu	6.5	6.5	6.5	7.5	7
10		Fri	7.5	7.5	7.5	5	7.5
11		Weekly hrs:	=SUM(C6:C10)	=SUM(D6:D10)	=SUM(E6:E10)	=SUM(F6:F10)	=SUM(G6:G10)
12							
13		Weekly pay:	=C11*$C$3	=D11*$C$3	=E11*$C$3	=F11*$C$3	=G11*$C$3

and then select **Trace Precedents** from the formulas menu, we can see the result as shown below:

	F13			f_x	=F11*$C$3	
	A	B	C	D	E	F	G

	A	B	C	D	E	F	G
1				Hours worked			
2							
3		Hourly Rate	£8.00			Date	05/05/2014
4							
5		Week Beg	1st Apr	8th Apr	15th Apr	22nd Apr	29th Apr
6		Mon	7	8.5	7	8	6.5
7		Tue	6.5	6.5	7	7.5	7.5
8		Wed	5.5	7.5	7	6	8
9		Thu	6.5	6.5	6.5	7.5	7
10		Fri	7.5	7.5	7.5	5	7.5
11		Weekly hrs:	33	36.5	35	34	36.5
12							
13		Weekly pay:	£264.00	£292.00	£280.00	£272.00	£292.00

From this image you can see that the arrows indicate that cells C3 and F11 affect (ie are precedents of) the cell F13.

If we were to select **Trace Precedents** for a second time without moving from the selected cell, we would see the cells which are precedents for F11, hence, F6,F7,F8,F9 and F10 are all identified, as shown below:

	F13			f_x	=F11*$C$3	
	A	B	C	D	E	F	G

	A	B	C	D	E	F	G
1				Hours worked			
2							
3		Hourly Rate	£8.00			Date	05/05/2014
4							
5		Week Beg	1st Apr	8th Apr	15th Apr	22nd Apr	29th Apr
6		Mon	7	8.5	7	8	6.5
7		Tue	6.5	6.5	7	7.5	7.5
8		Wed	5.5	7.5	7	6	8
9		Thu	6.5	6.5	6.5	7.5	7
10		Fri	7.5	7.5	7.5	5	7.5
11		Weekly hrs:	33	36.5	35	34	36.5
12							
13		Weekly pay:	£264.00	£292.00	£280.00	£272.00	£292.00

There are no arrows from C3, since it has no precedents.

The arrows show that F11 utilises the cells F6 through to F10.

This **Trace Precedents** tool is very useful for checking formulas, especially on more complex sheets.

To Trace Precedents for a particular cell:

- select the required cell
- select **Trace Precedents** from the menu bar (usually in the formulas section)
- repeat as required

To remove the arrows generated:

- select **Remove Arrows** from the menu bar

trace dependents

The **Trace Dependents** facility allows you to identify those cells which **are affected by** the value of the currently selected cell.

For example if cell D4 contained the formula

=22+F4/20

D4 would be a **dependent** of F4, because its value is dependent on the value of F4.

If we return to the Hours worked worksheet again and select cell C3, the Hourly Rate value, and then select **Trace Dependents**, the screen will appear as follows:

	C3		f_x	8		
	A	B	C	D	E	F	G
1			Hours worked				
2							
3		Hourly Rate	£8.00			Date	05/05/2014
4							
5		Week Beg	1st Apr	8th Apr	15th Apr	22nd Apr	29th Apr
6		Mon	7	8.5	7	8	6.5
7		Tue	6.5	6.5	7	7.5	7.5
8		Wed	5.5	7.5	7	6	8
9		Thu	6.5	6.5	6.5	7.5	7
10		Fri	7.5	7.5	7.5	5	7.5
11		Weekly hrs:	33	36.5	35	34	36.5
12							
13		Weekly pay:	£264.00	£292.00	£280.00	£272.00	£292.00

From this image you can see that the arrows indicate that cell C3 is used in the formulas in cells C13, D13, E13, F13 and G13 showing that cells C13 through to G13 are all **dependent** on C3.

If we were to select **Trace Dependents** for a second time without moving from the selected cell, there are no dependents on these cells, so no additional cells are identified.

However, if we had an additional column of Totals, as shown below…

	A	B	C	D	E	F	G	H
		H13			fx	=SUM(C13:G13)		
1				Hours worked				
2								
3		Hourly Rate	£8.00			Date	05/05/2014	
4								
5		Week Beg	1st Apr	8th Apr	15th Apr	22nd Apr	29th Apr	Totals
6		Mon	7	8.5	7	8	6.5	37
7		Tue	6.5	6.5	7	7.5	7.5	35
8		Wed	5.5	7.5	7	6	8	34
9		Thu	6.5	6.5	6.5	7.5	7	34
10		Fri	7.5	7.5	7.5	5	7.5	35
11		Weekly hrs:	33	36.5	35	34	36.5	175
12								
13		Weekly pay:	£264.00	£292.00	£280.00	£272.00	£292.00	£1,400.00

… and if we were to select C3, and **Trace Dependents**, once and then for a second time, we can see how H13 becomes highlighted, since it is dependent on C13 through to G13. This is illustrated above.

	A	B	C	D	E	F	G	H
1				Hours worked				
2								
3		Hourly Rate	£8.00			Date	05/05/2014	
4								
5		Week Beg	1st Apr	8th Apr	15th Apr	22nd Apr	29th Apr	Totals
6		Mon	7	8.5	7	8	6.5	37
7		Tue	6.5	6.5	7	7.5	7.5	35
8		Wed	5.5	7.5	7	6	8	34
9		Thu	6.5	6.5	6.5	7.5	7	34
10		Fri	7.5	7.5	7.5	5	7.5	35
11		Weekly hrs:	33	36.5	35	34	36.5	175
12								
13		Weekly pay:	£264.00	£292.00	£280.00	£272.00	£292.00	£1,400.00

To Trace Dependents for a particular cell:

■ select the required cell

- select **Trace Dependents** from the menu bar (usually in the formulas section)
- repeat as required

To remove the arrows generated:

- select **Remove Arrows** from the menu bar

WORKING WITH MULTIPLE WORKSHEETS

When creating a formula, it is possible to use or reference data **on another worksheet** within the same workbook by including the worksheet name, followed by an exclamation mark (!) within the formula.

If we look at the images below, we can see a simple workbook with four worksheets, named Quarter1, Jan, Feb and Mar.

	A	B	C	D	E	F	G
1	Quarterly Sales figures						
2							
3		Jan	Feb	Mar	Total		
4	Sales						
5							
6							
7							
8							

Quarter1 / Jan / Feb / Mar / Sheet4

Each of the monthly worksheets shows the details of sales for that month, together with a total, as can be seen in the image for the Jan sheet below.

	A	B	C	D	E	F
1	Month	Product	Value	Who	Country	
2	Jan	Accessories	£125.75	TP	IND	
3	Jan	Footwear	£99.95	SM	PKN	
4	Jan	Luggage	£220.00	IY	GER	
5	Jan	Luggage	£1,400.00	MP	UK	
6	Jan	Luggage	£1,400.00	MP	UK	
7						
8	Total		£3,245.70			

Quarter1 **Jan** / Feb / Mar / Sheet4

We want to display each of these totals on our Quarter1 sheet, so that we have a summary of the monthly sales and can total across the three months.

In this case we want cell B4 on worksheet Quarter1, to contain the total value for Jan, found in cell C8 on worksheet Jan. To do this:

■ move to cell B4 on worksheet Quarter1

■ enter = (to indicate a formula)

■ move to cell C8 on worksheet Jan

■ press **RETURN** to complete the formula

Looking at the image below we can see the formula created in cell B4 in the formula bar of worksheet Quarter1:

=Jan!C8

	B4	▾			*fx*	=Jan!C8	
	A	B	C	D	E	F	G
1	Quarterly Sales figures						
2							
3		Jan	Feb	Mar	Total		
4	Sales	£3,245.70					
5							
6							
7							
8							

Quarter1 / Jan / Feb / Mar / Sheet4

The formula contains a direct reference to the work sheet **Jan**, followed by an exclamation mark (!) to indicate that this is a worksheet name, and then the cell reference C8 in the worksheet Jan. We would repeat this for each of the other months in the quarter. This is shown below:

	D4	▾			*fx*	=Mar!C9	
	A	B	C	D	E	F	G
1	Quarterly Sales figures						
2							
3		Jan	Feb	Mar	Total		
4	Sales	£3,245.70	£1,822.65	£731.35	£5,799.70		
5							
6							
7							
8							

Quarter1 / Jan / Feb / Mar / Sheet4

moving or copying a worksheet

In our Quarterly Sales workbook, suppose we want to copy the March (Mar) worksheet, to create the one for April, it is very simple to make a copy of a worksheet:

- select the worksheet you want to copy
- right click on the worksheet name tab
- select **Move** or **Copy**

The Move or copy options will be displayed, as shown below:

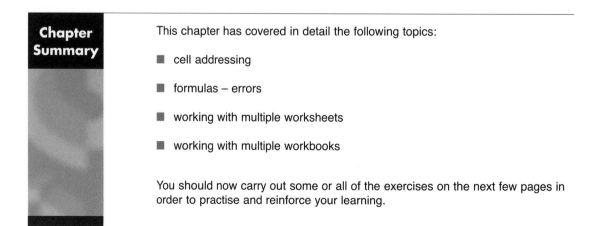

- choose where the copy sheet is to be placed in the workbook, in this case before Sheet4, and after Mar
- select the **Create a copy** check box, so that it is ticked, since we want to keep the original sheet
- press OK

<table>
<tr><td>**Chapter Summary**</td><td>This chapter has covered in detail the following topics:</td></tr>
</table>

- cell addressing

- formulas – errors

- working with multiple worksheets

- working with multiple workbooks

You should now carry out some or all of the exercises on the next few pages in order to practise and reinforce your learning.

Activities

Exercise 1 – cell addressing and error checking

In this first exercise we are going to calculate weekly pay for a group of employees based on the hours they have worked. We will be using absolute cell addressing.

Stage 1

In this stage we start to create some formulas.

1. Download the file **Ch6WeeklyPay**.
2. Save this workbook with the name **Ch6Exercise1**.

The workbook should look as shown below:

◢	A	B	C	D	E	F
1	Weekly Pay data					
2						
3	Std weekly hours	38				
4	Hourly Rate	£8.50				
5	Overtime Rate	£10.50				
6						
7	Employee	Hours worked	Overtime hours	Basic pay	Overtime pay	Total pay
8	Johal	40				
9	Jones	38				
10	Wakula	50				
11	White	52				
12	Hacek	38				
13	Bhopal	49				
14	Plant	39.5				

First we are going to make some format changes.

3. Format columns D, E and F to be **currency** with £ symbol and 2 decimal places.
4. Centre the headings in row 7, columns B through F.
5. Enter a formula in cell C8 to **calculate** the **Overtime hours** for Johal using **Hours worked** (B8) and **Std weekly hours** (cell B3) and absolute addressing in your formula.
6. Copy this formula for the other employees (cells C9 through to C14).

Your workbook should look as shown below:

	A	B	C	D	E	F
1	Weekly Pay data					
2						
3	Std weekly hours	38				
4	Hourly Rate	£8.50				
5	Overtime Rate	£10.50				
6						
7	Employee	Hours worked	Overtime hours	Basic pay	Overtime pay	Total pay
8	Johal	40	2			
9	Jones	38	0			
10	Wakula	50	12			
11	White	52	14			
12	Hacek	38	0			
13	Bhopal	49	11			
14	Plant	39.5	1.5			

7. Select **show formulas** so that your formulas are displayed.

The first 4 columns of your workbook should look similar to:

C8   ▼ f_x =B8-$B$3

	A	B	C	D
1	Weekly Pay data			
2				
3	Std weekly hours	38		
4	Hourly Rate	8.5		
5	Overtime Rate	10.5		
6				
7	Employee	Hours worked	Overtime hours	Basic pay
8	Johal	40	=B8-$B$3	
9	Jones	38	=B9-$B$3	
10	Wakula	50	=B10-$B$3	
11	White	52	=B11-$B$3	
12	Hacek	38	=B12-$B$3	
13	Bhopal	49	=B13-$B$3	
14	Plant	39.5	=B14-$B$3	

8. Turn off show formulas.

9. Save your workbook.

Stage 2

We are going to continue creating formulas, and improving the spreadsheet.

1. Enter the formula in cell **D8**, to calculate **Basic pay** for Johal including cell B4 in your formula and using absolute addressing.

2. Enter the formula in cell **E8**, to calculate **Overtime pay** for Johal including cell B5 in your formula and using absolute addressing.

3. Copy the formulas in D8 and E8 for the other employees.

4. Enter the formulas for total pay in column F for all employees.

5. Save your workbook.

Your workbook should look as shown below:

	A	B	C	D	E	F
1	Weekly Pay data					
2						
3	Std weekly hours	38				
4	Hourly Rate	£8.50				
5	Overtime Rate	£10.50				
6						
7	Employee	Hours worked	Overtime hours	Basic pay	Overtime pay	Total pay
8	Johal	40	2	£323.00	£21.00	£344.00
9	Jones	38	0	£323.00	£0.00	£323.00
10	Wakula	50	12	£323.00	£126.00	£449.00
11	White	52	14	£323.00	£147.00	£470.00
12	Hacek	38	0	£323.00	£0.00	£323.00
13	Bhopal	49	11	£323.00	£115.50	£438.50
14	Plant	39.5	1.5	£323.00	£15.75	£338.75

6. Select **show formulas**.

Your worksheet should look similar to the image on the next page:

	A	B	C	D	E	F
1	Weekly Pay da					
2						
3	Std weekly hours	38				
4	Hourly Rate	8.5				
5	Overtime Rate	10.5				
6						
7	Employee	Hours worked	Overtime hours	Basic pay	Overtime pay	Total pay
8	Johal	40	=B8-$B$3	=$B$3 *$B$4	=C8*$B$5	=D8+E8
9	Jones	38	=B9-$B$3	=$B$3 *$B$4	=C9*$B$5	=D9+E9
10	Wakula	50	=B10-$B$3	=$B$3 *$B$4	=C10*$B$5	=D10+E10
11	White	52	=B11-$B$3	=$B$3 *$B$4	=C11*$B$5	=D11+E11
12	Hacek	38	=B12-$B$3	=$B$3 *$B$4	=C12*$B$5	=D12+E12
13	Bhopal	49	=B13-$B$3	=$B$3 *$B$4	=C13*$B$5	=D13+E13
14	Plant	39.5	=B14-$B$3	=$B$3 *$B$4	=C14*$B$5	=D14+E14

7.   Turn off **show formulas**.

Stage 3

We are going to check our formulas within the spreadsheet.

1.   Change the formula in cell F11 to be =D11-E11.

2.   Perform an **error check** on the whole worksheet.

The **Inconsistent Formula** warning screen shown below should appear:

Error Checking	? ✕
Error in cell F11 =D11-E11	Copy Formula from Above
Inconsistent Formula	Help on this error
The formula in this cell differs from the formulas in this area of the spreadsheet.	Ignore Error
	Edit in Formula Bar
Options...	Previous Next

3. Since we have deliberately introduced this error, select **Copy Formula from Above** to correct the formula.

4. Select cell B3, and choose **Trace Dependents**.

The dependency arrows are shown below:

5. Remove the arrows.

6. Change the formula in cell D14 to be =B14*$B$4.

7. Again, select cell B3, and choose **Trace Dependents**.

The dependency arrows are shown below:

This highlights the fact that the formula in cell D14 is no longer using cell B3 (Std weekly hours)

8. Remove the arrows.

9. Correct the formula.

10. To confirm our correction, select cell D14 and **Trace Precedents**.

The precedent arrows are shown below:

	A	B	C	D	E	F
1	Weekly Pay data					
2						
3	Std weekly hours	38				
4	Hourly Rate	£8.50				
5	Overtime Rate	£10.50				
6						
7	Employee	Hours worked	Overtime hours	Basic pay	Overtime pay	Total pay
8	Johal	40	2	£323.00	£21.00	£344.00
9	Jones	38	0	£323.00	£0.00	£323.00
10	Wakula	50	12	£323.00	£126.00	£449.00
11	White	52	14	£323.00	£147.00	£470.00
12	Hacek	38	0	£323.00	£0.00	£323.00
13	Bhopal	49	11	£323.00	£115.50	£438.50
14	Plant	39.5	1.5	£323.00	£15.75	£338.75

Exercise 2 – working with multiple worksheets

In this exercise we will move data and formulas from one worksheet to another and to worksheets in another workbook. We are going to make use of an existing spreadsheet, which contains data relating to monthly car sales.

Stage 1

In this stage we are going to use **Move or Copy worksheets** within the same workbook.

1. Download the file **Ch6Carsales**.

2. Save this workbook with the name **Ch6Exercise2**.

The workbook should look as shown below:

⊿	A	B	C	D	E	F	G	H
1	Car Sales							
2								
3		Totals	Month1	Month2	Month3	Month4	Month5	Month6
4	Ford	190,000	25,090	25,000	60,000	25,010	30,900	24,000
5	Volkswagen	98,510	13,200	6,150	32,900	15,130	15,040	16,090
6	Hyundai	9,000	1,000	1,500	2,500	1,000	1,000	2,000
7	Skoda	15,400	1,200	2,800	4,000	3,500	2,130	1,770
8	Kia	13,360	930	1,050	5,430	1,500	2,110	2,340
9	Renault	94,820	7,000	32,090	25,600	9,230	9,100	11,800
10	Vauxhall	166,750	22,000	10,500	55,000	25,050	24,100	30,100

Car Sales / Sheet2 / Sheet3

3. Select cell B4, note the formula:

   =SUM(C4:H4)

4. Create a copy of the Car Sales worksheet, using **Move or Copy** worksheet and position it directly after the **Car Sales** worksheet.

5. Select cell B4 on the worksheet copy. You will see the formula **=SUM(C4:H4)** in the formula bar, click in the formula bar and all cells used in this formula will be highlighted.

6. Save your workbook.

Your workbook should look as shown on the next page.

	SUM	▼	● × ✓ fx	=SUM(C4:H4)			
◢	A	B	C	SUM(**number1**, [number2], ...)		G	H
1	Car Sales						
2							
3		Totals	*Month1*	*Month2*	*Month3*	*Month4*	*Month5*	*Month6*
4	Ford	=SUM(C4:H4)	25,090	25,000	60,000	25,010	30,900	24,000
5	Volkswagen	98,510	13,200	6,150	32,900	15,130	15,040	16,090
6	Hyundai	9,000	1,000	1,500	2,500	1,000	1,000	2,000
7	Skoda	15,400	1,200	2,800	4,000	3,500	2,130	1,770
8	Kia	13,360	930	1,050	5,430	1,500	2,110	2,340
9	Renault	94,820	7,000	32,090	25,600	9,230	9,100	11,800
10	Vauxhall	166,750	22,000	10,500	55,000	25,050	24,100	30,100

I◀ ◀ ▶ ▶I   Car Sales   **Car Sales (2)**   Sheet2   Sheet3 ◀ | ▶

You can see that all the data and the formulas have been copied onto the new worksheet – Car Sales (2).

Stage 2

This stage involves moving data from one worksheet to another using copy and paste.

1. Check that you have another worksheet in the workbook you have open; if not add a worksheet (as described in Chapter 1) and name it **Car Sales Paste**.

2. Select all the data on the Car Sales worksheet, select **Copy** (using the menu, or **CTRL** and **C**).

3. Select worksheet **Car Sales Paste**, move to cell B2, select **Paste**, the data from **Car Sales** will be pasted onto the worksheet **Car Sales Paste**.

4. On worksheet **Car Sales Paste**, make Column A four units wide.

5. On worksheet **Car Sales Paste**, move to cell C5. You should see the formula for the Total for the Ford row (now Row 5 on this sheet):

    =SUM(D5:I5)

This has been modified to reflect the new row and column position, as shown in the image at the top of the next page.

	C5			f_x	=SUM(D5:I5)				
	A	B	C	D	E	F	G	H	I
1									
2		Car Sales							
3									
4			Totals	Month1	Month2	Month3	Month4	Month5	Month6
5		Ford	190,000	25,090	25,000	60,000	25,010	30,900	24,000
6		Volkswagen	98,510	13,200	6,150	32,900	15,130	15,040	16,090
7		Hyundai	9,000	1,000	1,500	2,500	1,000	1,000	2,000
8		Skoda	15,400	1,200	2,800	4,000	3,500	2,130	1,770
9		Kia	13,360	930	1,050	5,430	1,500	2,110	2,340
10		Renault	94,820	7,000	32,090	25,600	9,230	9,100	11,800
11		Vauxhall	166,750	22,000	10,500	55,000	25,050	24,100	30,100

6. Save your workbook.

Exercise 3 – working with multiple workbooks

In this stage we are going to use **Move or Copy worksheets** to combine worksheets from two different workbooks. Both workbooks contain sales figures, which we will use to produce totals for 12 months.

1. Download the file **Ch6Salesfirst**.

2. Save this workbook with the same name **Ch6first**.

The workbook should look as shown below:

	A	B	C	D	E	F	G	H
1	Car Sales		Months 1 to 6					
2								
3			Totals	Month1	Month2	Month3	Month4	Month5	Month6
4	Ford		190,000	25,090	25,000	60,000	25,010	30,900	24,000
5	Volkswagen		98,510	13,200	6,150	32,900	15,130	15,040	16,090
6	Hyundai		9,000	1,000	1,500	2,500	1,000	1,000	2,000
7	Skoda		15,400	1,200	2,800	4,000	3,500	2,130	1,770
8	Kia		13,360	930	1,050	5,430	1,500	2,110	2,340
9	Renault		94,820	7,000	32,090	25,600	9,230	9,100	11,800
10	Vauxhall		166,750	22,000	10,500	55,000	25,050	24,100	30,100
11								

Sales 1-6 / Sheet2 / Sheet3

3. Download the file **Ch6Salessecond**.

4. Save this workbook with the same name **Ch6second**.

The workbook should look as shown below:

	A	B	C	D	E	F	G	H
1	Car Sales			Months 7-12				
2								
3		Totals	Month7	Month8	Month9	Month10	Month11	Month12
4	Ford	193,800	25,592	25,500	61,200	25,510	31,518	24,480
5	Volkswagen	100,480	13,464	6,273	33,558	15,433	15,341	16,412
6	Hyundai	9,180	1,020	1,530	2,550	1,020	1,020	2,040
7	Skoda	15,708	1,224	2,856	4,080	3,570	2,173	1,805
8	Kia	13,627	949	1,071	5,539	1,530	2,152	2,387
9	Renault	96,716	7,140	32,732	26,112	9,415	9,282	12,036
10	Vauxhall	173,350	28,600	10,500	55,000	25,050	24,100	30,100
11								

Sales 7-12 / Sheet2 / Sheet3

Now we have both workbooks, we are going to place both sheets into **Ch6first**, create a totals page, and save the combined workbook with a new name.

5. If not already open, open both workbooks.

6. Select workbook **Ch6second**.

7. Select worksheet **Sales 7-12**, using **move or copy**, copy this worksheet to workbook **Ch6first**, **after** worksheet **Sales 1-6**.

Your **Ch6first** workbook should look as shown below:

	A	B	C	D	E	F	G	H
1	Car Sales			Months 7-12				
2								
3		Totals	Month7	Month8	Month9	Month10	Month11	Month12
4	Ford	193,800	25,592	25,500	61,200	25,510	31,518	24,480
5	Volkswagen	100,480	13,464	6,273	33,558	15,433	15,341	16,412
6	Hyundai	9,180	1,020	1,530	2,550	1,020	1,020	2,040
7	Skoda	15,708	1,224	2,856	4,080	3,570	2,173	1,805
8	Kia	13,627	949	1,071	5,539	1,530	2,152	2,387
9	Renault	96,716	7,140	32,732	26,112	9,415	9,282	12,036
10	Vauxhall	173,350	28,600	10,500	55,000	25,050	24,100	30,100
11								

Sales 1-6 / **Sales 7-12** / Sheet2 / Sheet3

8. Select **Ch6first** workbook.

9. Rename worksheet Sheet2 as **Totals**.

10. Move worksheet **Totals** before worksheet Sales 1-6.

11. Save your workbook as **Ch6totals**.

◢	A	B	C	D	E	F	G	H	I
1									
2									
3									
4									
5									
6									
7									
8									
9									
10									
11									

◄ ◄ ► ►| **Totals** / Sales 1-6 / Sales 7-12 / Sheet3 / 🖑| ◄ [　　　　　　IIII　　　　　　] ►

Stage 2

We are now going to format the Totals sheet and introduce some formulas to combine the car sales totals for each model from the two detailed sales sheets.

1. Select **Ch6totals** workbook.

2. Select worksheet **Sales 1-6**.

3. **Copy** cells A1 through to A10, and paste on worksheet **Totals** starting in cell A1.

4. Widen column A to 12, format column B to currency £, no decimal places.

5. Change the text in cell A1 to Total Car Sales.

6. Move to cell B4 on the **Totals** worksheet. We are going to create the first formula:

   a. enter = to indicate a formula

   b. select worksheet Sales 1-6

   c. select cell B4

   d. enter + (plus sign)

   e. select worksheet Sales 7-12

   f. select cell B4

   g. press ENTER (or RETURN)

Looking at the formula, you can see the references to each of the sheets and the appropriate cells as shown in the image below:

B4		▾		*fx*	='Sales 1-6'!B4+'Sales 7-12 '!B4		
◢	**A**	**B**	**C**	**D**	**E**	**F**	**G**
1	Total Car Sales						
2							
3							
4	Ford	£383,800					
5	Volkswagen						
6	Hyundai						
7	Skoda						
8	Kia						
9	Renault						
10	Vauxhall						

7.   Repeat for each of the other totals in column B on the **Totals** worksheet.

8.   Save your workbook.

It should appear as shown below:

B10		▾		*fx*	='Sales 1-6'!B10+'Sales 7-12 '!B10		
◢	**A**	**B**	**C**	**D**	**E**	**F**	**G**
1	Total Car Sales						
2							
3							
4	Ford	£383,800					
5	Volkswagen	£198,990					
6	Hyundai	£18,180					
7	Skoda	£31,108					
8	Kia	£26,987					
9	Renault	£191,536					
10	Vauxhall	£340,100					

You have now completed the exercises for this chapter.

7 Creating charts, sorting and checking data

this chapter covers...

This chapter covers how to sort and filter your data for easier analysis, check for spelling errors and create a variety of charts.

The concepts and techniques covered are:

- *spellcheck*

- *sorting data*

- *filter data*

- *types of charts*

- *creating charts*

SPELLCHECK

Spreadsheet packages usually provide built-in **Spellchecking** tools to check the text in your worksheets.

For our example, we will use a modified version of our expenditure forecast worksheet, which now contains several typing mistakes. This is illustrated below:

A1			f_x	Expenditure forecsat			

◢	A	B	C	D	E	F	G	H
1	Expenditure forecsat							
2								
3								
4		January	February	March	April	May	June	Average
5	Salaries	£80,000	£80,000	£80,000	£90,000	£90,000	£90,000	£85,000
6	Insurance	£1,000	£500	£0	£0	£0	£500	£333
7	Accountanci	£270	£0	£270	£0	£270	£0	£135
8	Advertising	£0	£1,500	£0	£0	£0	£1,800	£550
9	Psotage	£95	£190	£95	£80	£95	£150	£118
10	Rent	£3,500	£3,500	£3,500	£3,500	£3,500	£3,500	£3,500
11	Stationery	£57	£90	£0	£90	£0	£90	£55
12	Totals	£84,922	£85,780	£83,865	£93,670	£93,865	£96,040	

If we select **Spelling** (or **Spellcheck**) from the Review menu, the first text to be identified will be in cell A1, where we have spelt forecast incorrectly:

Not in Dictionary:

forecsat   Ignore Once

Ignore All

Add to Dictionary

Suggestions:

forecast   Change

Change All

AutoCorrect

Dictionary language: English (U.K.)

Options...   Undo Last   Cancel

Once identified, you can choose how you want to proceed from the options given, as shown above. The tool can step through and check the spelling in all cells on the worksheet.

Within the spellcheck tool options, you can choose rules which you want to apply when performing a spellcheck – for example, to ignore words that are all upper case.

To set your rule choices for Spellcheck:

- select **Options** from the appropriate menu
- select **Proofing**
- check or uncheck the rules to configure as you require

You can request **Spellcheck** on just one cell or a **group of cells**.

To perform Spellcheck on a cell or group of cells:

- select the required cell(s)
- select **Spellcheck** (or its equivalent) from the menu

The rules will be applied as set up in the Options/Proofing described above, and any cells with a spelling error will be highlighted and suggestions for revised spellings offered.

SORTING DATA

If we look at the workbook we worked in the last chapter – Weekly Pay data, shown in the image below, we can see that the employee names are not in alphabetical order.

⬙	A	B	C	D	E	F
1	Weekly Pay data					
2						
3	Std weekly hours	38				
4	Hourly Rate	£8.60				
5	Overtime Rate	£10.75				
6						
7	Employee	Hours worked	Overtime hours	Basic pay	Overtime pay	Total pay
8	Johal	40	2	£326.80	£21.50	£348.30
9	Jones	38	0	£326.80	£0.00	£326.80
10	Wakula	50	12	£326.80	£129.00	£455.80
11	White	52	14	£326.80	£150.50	£477.30
12	Hacek	38	0	£326.80	£0.00	£326.80
13	Bhopal	49	11	£326.80	£118.25	£445.05
14	Plant	39.5	1.5	£326.80	£16.13	£342.93

Alphabetical sorting is very simple, using a built-in **sort tool**, which allows us to sort data alphabetically A to Z, or reversely Z to A. Numeric data can also be sorted in ascending or descending order.

When we are sorting data, we have to identify and select the data which is to be sorted. It is very important that we include any associated data in the nearby columns within our selection.

In the example below, because the data in the hours and pay columns is specific to the individual employee, if we change the order of the employees, we must also change the order of the other data in the same way. This will happen automatically if we include the associated columns in our selection, before we select sort.

In the image below, the data in all six columns is selected.

7	Employee	Hours worked	Overtime hours	Basic pay	Overtime pay	Total pay
8	Johal	40	2	£326.80	£21.50	£348.30
9	Jones	38	0	£326.80	£0.00	£326.80
10	Wakula	50	12	£326.80	£129.00	£455.80
11	White	52	14	£326.80	£150.50	£477.30
12	Hacek	38	0	£326.80	£0.00	£326.80
13	Bhopal	49	11	£326.80	£118.25	£445.05
14	Plant	39.5	1.5	£326.80	£16.13	£342.93

We then select **Sort and Filter** from the Home menu, choose order alphabetically A to Z and get the results below:

7	Employee	Hours worked	Overtime hours	Basic pay	Overtime pay	Total pay
8	Bhopal	49	11	£326.80	£118.25	£445.05
9	Hacek	38	0	£326.80	£0.00	£326.80
10	Johal	40	2	£326.80	£21.50	£348.30
11	Jones	38	0	£326.80	£0.00	£326.80
12	Plant	39.5	1.5	£326.80	£16.13	£342.93
13	Wakula	50	12	£326.80	£129.00	£455.80
14	White	52	14	£326.80	£150.50	£477.30

The selected data has been sorted by the first column on the left – **Employee,** and you can see that all the data has moved with the individual employee name and remains correct. The data will always be sorted by the first column on the left, unless you use **Custom Sort** as described below.

Columns containing numbers can be sorted in **Ascending** (increasing) or **Descending** (decreasing) order.

In summary, to sort data:

- **select** the data which we want to sort (including any associated data)
- select **Sort and Filter** from the menu
- choose the **order** (A to Z, Z to A, Ascending or Descending) as appropriate

custom sort

To sort the data by a column other than the first column on the left, select **Custom Sort** from the Sort and filter menu. You can then choose a different column from the list, as can be seen in the image below.

You would normally choose to **Sort On** Values, and select **Order** as required.

FILTER DATA

If you have a spreadsheet containing a large number of rows of data as in the example opposite (which shows car sales by month), the **Filter** facility allows you to filter the data so that you only see rows which contain certain values or combinations of values. For example **Filter** could show just those rows where Region=North West or a combination such as Region=North West and Manufacturer=Ford.

To **Filter** data:

- select the cell containing the leftmost heading text
- select **Filter** from the **Sort and Filter** menu.

You will see something similar to the lower image on the opposite page, with the drop-down symbols next to the text at the top of each column.

◢	A	B	C	D	E	F
1	**Year**	**Month**	**Manufacturer**	**Type**	**Region**	**Quantity**
2	2015	Feb	Ford	T	South	1,500
3	2015	Feb	Seat	I	East	220
4	2015	Mar	Seat	I	South West	155
5	2015	Apr	VW	O	North West	35
6	2015	Mar	Mercedes	M	North West	125
7	2015	Jan	BMW	T	South	126
8	2015	Mar	Toyota	I	East	45
9	2015	Jul	VW	O	South West	56
10	2015	Feb	Ford	O	South West	68
11	2015	Jan	Seat	M	South	100
12	2015	Apr	Seat	T	South	1,460
13	2015	Aug	VW	I	East	1,500
14	2013	Jan	Mercedes	I	South West	220
15	2013	Mar	BMW	O	North West	155
16	2013	Feb	Toyota	M	North West	35
17	2013	Jun	VW	T	South	125
18	2013	Jul	Ford	I	East	126
19	2013	Jul	BMW	O	South West	45
20	2013	Apr	VW	O	South West	56
21	2013	Aug	Mercedes	M	South	68
22	2013	Aug	Toyota	T	South	100
23	2014	Sep	BMW	I	East	1,460
24	2014	Sep	BMW	I	South West	34
25	2014	Apr	Ford	O	North West	56
26	2014	Nov	Seat	M	North West	125
27	2014	Nov	Seat	T	South	126
28	2014	Nov	VW	I	East	45
29	2014	Dec	Mercedes	O	South West	56

◢	A	B	C	D	E	F
1	**Year** ▾	**Month** ▾	**Manufacturer** ▾	**Type** ▾	**Region** ▾	**Quantit** ▾
2	2015	Feb	Ford	T	South	1,500
3	2015	Feb	Seat	I	East	220
4	2015	Mar	Seat	I	South West	155
5	2015	Apr	VW	O	North West	35
6	2015	Mar	Mercedes	M	North West	125
7	2015	Jan	BMW	T	South	126
8	2015	Mar	Toyota	I	East	45

You can now choose how you want to filter the data:

- click on the drop-down arrow on a column
- select the required values which you wish to analyse from the drop-down menu
- repeat for other columns as required to refine the rows displayed

In the image below, you can see the rows which would be displayed when a filter of Region=North West is applied to the sales data. The funnel symbol next to **Region** indicates that a filter has been applied to that column.

	A	B	C	D	E	F
1	Year ▾	Month ▾	Manufacturer ▾	Type ▾	Region ⊤	Quantit ▾
5	2015	Apr	VW	O	North West	35
6	2015	Mar	Mercedes	M	North West	125
15	2013	Mar	BMW	O	North West	155
16	2013	Feb	Toyota	M	North West	35
25	2014	Apr	Ford	O	North West	56
26	2014	Nov	Seat	M	North West	125
33	2015	Dec	Ford	P	North West	34
35	2015	Dec	VW	O	North West	1,500
36	2015	Nov	Mercedes	O	North West	220

If we applied a further filter to the Manufacturer, looking only for Ford, we would get only those rows displayed where Region=North West and Manufacturer=Ford, as can be seen below:

	A	B	C	D	E	F
1	Year ▾	Month ▾	Manufacturer ⊤	Type ▾	Region ⊤	Quantit ▾
25	2014	Apr	Ford	O	North West	56
33	2015	Dec	Ford	P	North West	34

To turn off the active filter on a column:

- click on the Filter symbol on the column
- select **Clear Filters**

To remove all filters:

- select **Filter** from the **Sort and Filter** menu

(The filter icon will be highlighted in the menu, showing filtering is active.)

TYPES OF CHARTS

Within spreadsheet packages, there are a variety of different **chart** types available for the visual representation of data. In this section we are going to illustrate the following types of chart. Instructions for the creation of charts will follow in a separate section at the end of this chapter.

■ Bar or Column

■ Line

■ Pie

bar chart

The bar chart is probably the most commonly used chart, and can be applied to data that is arranged in columns or rows on a worksheet.

In the image below, you can see that we have taken six months of sales data, represented as a **vertical** bar chart, also known as **column** chart, showing how the value of sales has changed over the period of six months.

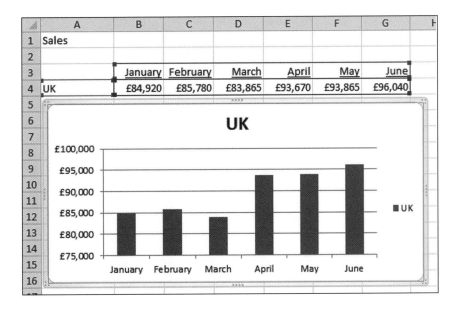

This is a bar chart in its simplest form, with only one set of data values. With two sets of data, sales in the UK and sales in China, we can show the values side by side.

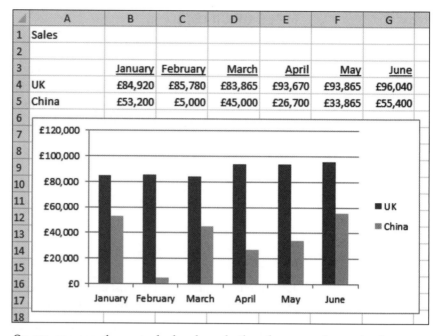

Or we can see them stacked, where both values are shown in the same column, as illustrated below:

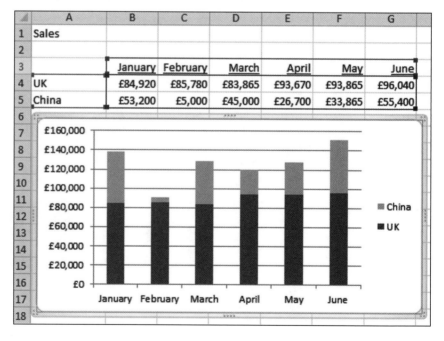

Bar charts can also be created with **horizontal** bars, as shown in the example on the next page.

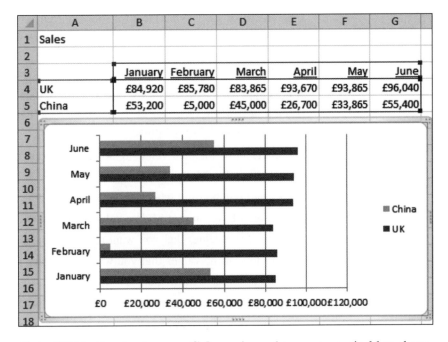

Note: Within the **chart** menu, **Column** is used to create vertical bar charts, and **Bar** to create horizontal bar charts.

line chart

Using the daily Share Price data which we looked at in Chapter 4 exercises, we can create a line chart showing the price of the share over a period of 20 days, as shown below:

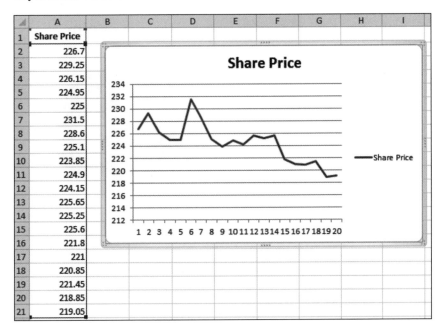

Line charts (or graphs) are ideal for showing trends in data over time and can be created from data that is arranged in columns or rows on a worksheet.

pie chart

A **pie chart** can be produced for only one set of data values, arranged in one column or row on a worksheet. It is known as a 'pie chart' because it looks like a pie divided into a number of 'slices'.

Pie charts show the data values relative to the total of the values. Each data value is shown in a pie chart as a percentage or proportion of the whole 'pie'.

A pie chart can be used when:

- you only have one set of data values that you want to plot
- none of the values that you want to plot are negative
- very few of the values that you want to plot are zero
- you do not have more than seven values
- the data values represent all the parts of the whole

In the image below you can see an example of a pie chart where the values represent sales in China for each of the six months:

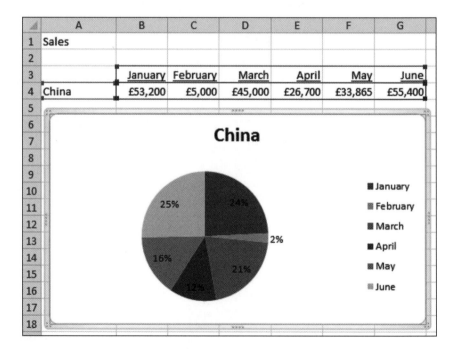

Each value is also shown as a percentage of the whole, which would be the total sales for the six months.

To make the pie chart more visual, it is possible to select a **3D** chart and the slices will be shown as three dimensional, or **exploded** where the individual slices are separated. These options can add to a chart's clarity.

The China sales data is shown as an exploded pie chart in the image below.

	A	B	C	D	E	F	G
1	Sales						
2							
3		January	February	March	April	May	June
4	China	£53,200	£5,000	£45,000	£26,700	£33,865	£55,400

CREATING CHARTS

We have seen that there are numerous chart types available to use. However the basic steps which can be used to create a chart from a worksheet are applicable to most chart types:

- select the data and headings on the worksheet to be presented in the chart
- select the chart type required
- enter a title and 'y' axis label for the chart
- label the 'x' axis to reflect the data shown (if applicable)

These steps are described and illustrated on the next page, using the sales data for UK and China.

◢	A	B	C	D	E	F	G
1	Sales						
2							
3		January	February	March	April	May	June
4	UK	£84,920	£85,780	£83,865	£93,670	£93,865	£96,040
5	China	£53,200	£5,000	£45,000	£26,700	£33,865	£55,400

You may wish to create a spreadsheet, and enter this data yourself, so that you can follow the steps through.

Step 1 – select the data

Select the data, including the text which relates to the data. We are going to select both rows of data, since we want to compare the two rows of sales values.

The data can be selected as shown below:

◢	A	B	C	D	E	F	G
1	Sales						
2							
3		January	February	March	April	May	June
4	UK	£84,920	£85,780	£83,865	£93,670	£93,865	£96,040
5	China	£53,200	£5,000	£45,000	£26,700	£33,865	£55,400

Note that in some versions of software, you may be taken through the chart creation by a 'help wizard', and may need to specify the range of your data.

This can be done by either moving to the data and selecting as shown in the image above, or manually specifying the range, in this case $A$3:$G$5, always using absolute cell addresses.

Step 2 – create the chart

Select **Insert chart** from the menu and then the type of chart required. In this example we are going to create a line chart to represent both rows of data.

A chart is created on the same worksheet by default.

In the image at the top of the next page, we have created a line chart, and placed it below our rows of data. Each row of data is also known as a **series**.

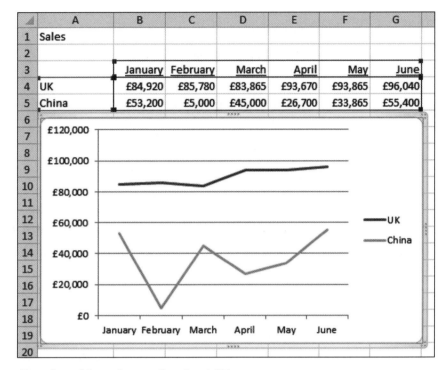

Step 3 – add or change the chart title

The chart axes are automatically created with scales based on the ranges of values in the data. The key (**legend**), which identifies which line on the graph represents which series of data, is shown to the right by default.

To introduce a title for the chart:

■ select the chart (single or double click)

■ from the **Chart tools menu**, select the **Layout** tab

■ select **Chart title**

■ at present this will show none, so select **Above chart**

The text **Chart Title** for the Chart appears, as shown below:

◢	A	B	C	D	E	F	G
1	Sales						
2							
3		January	February	March	April	May	June
4	UK	£84,920	£85,780	£83,865	£93,670	£93,865	£96,040
5	China	£53,200	£5,000	£45,000	£26,700	£33,865	£55,400
6							
7				**Chart Title**			
8							
9	£120,000						

It is very simple to change this text, by clicking the title text and entering the required title.

We will enter the title 'Sales figures'.

Step 4 – dealing with the 'y' axis (vertical axis)

The chart layout we have used does not include an axis label for the y axis. To add this manually:

- select the chart (single or double click)
- from the **Chart menu**, select the **Layout** tab
- select **Axis Titles**, **Primary Vertical Axis** title
- at present this will show none, so select **Rotated Title**
- edit the 'y' axis label as required – here 'Sales Value' is the chosen axis title

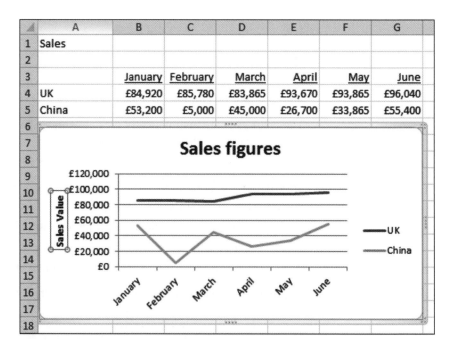

Step 5 – dealing with the 'x' axis (horizontal axis)

The layout we have used does not include an axis label for the x axis. To add this manually:

- select the chart (single or double click)
- from the **Chart menu**, select the **Layout** tab
- select **Axis Titles**, **Primary Horizontal Axis** title

■ at present this will show none, so select **Title below Axis**

■ edit the 'x' axis label as required – here 'Month' is the chosen axis title

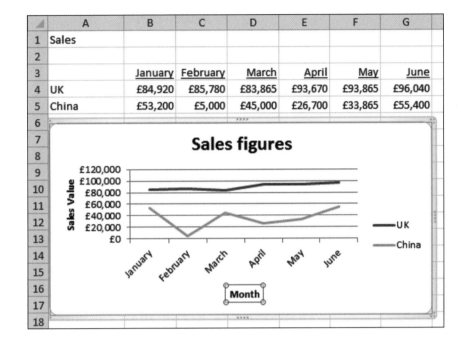

Step 6 – dealing with chart legend

The legend lists the name and the colour used to represent each data series in the chart. It is usually automatically added to the chart when the chart is created. It is possible to choose whether or not a legend should be displayed and if so, where it should be positioned within the chart.

To manipulate the chart legend:

■ select the chart (single or double click)

■ from the **Chart menu**, select the **Layout** tab

■ select **Legend**

■ choose options from the **Legend menu** as required

In the previous image, you can see the legend is positioned on the right of the chart, and in the image on the next page, it is positioned to the left of the chart.

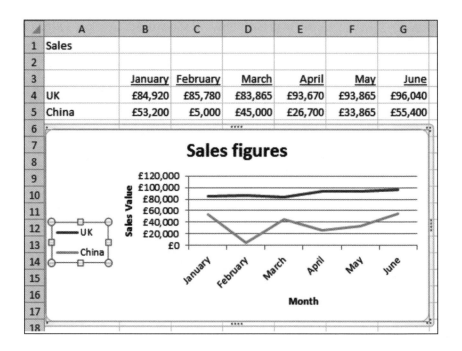

changing the graph type for one data series

Once we have created our chart representing our data, it is possible to change how one of the sets of data is shown on the chart. For example, we may want to show the data from China as a bar chart, still keeping the UK sales as a line graph.

To do this:

- right click on the line representing the China data on the chart (each data point will be highlighted)
- select **Design** from the **Chart Tools** menu
- select **Change Chart Type**
- select **Column** and OK

The chart should now look as shown in the image on the next page:

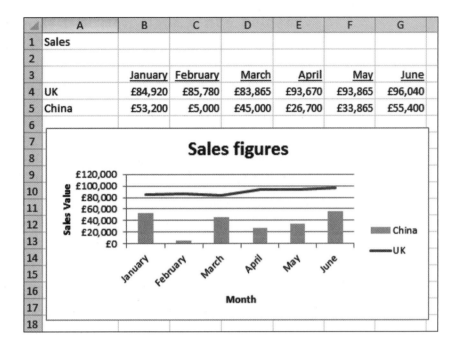

	A	B	C	D	E	F	G
1	Sales						
2							
3		January	February	March	April	May	June
4	UK	£84,920	£85,780	£83,865	£93,670	£93,865	£96,040
5	China	£53,200	£5,000	£45,000	£26,700	£33,865	£55,400

moving or resizing

Once you have created a chart as described in the previous steps, you may wish to resize or move the chart to a different location either on the same or a different worksheet, for example to avoid it covering some of the data.

To resize a chart:

▪ click on the chart to select it

▪ place the cursor over one of the corners of the chart frame, or the dots around the edges of the frame (you will see the cursor changes to a double headed arrow)

▪ click and drag to the required size

To move a chart:

▪ click on the chart to select it

▪ click and drag the chart to its new position

If you want to move the chart to a new worksheet:

▪ right click within the space surrounding the chart, but still within the chart frame

▪ select **Move chart** from the menu

▪ select the worksheet to which the chart is to move

changing how a chart item is displayed

To change the properties of an item on the chart such as Chart Title or axis label, if you **right** click on the item you will get a menu allowing you to change how the item is displayed or formatted.

labelling a pie chart

In the case of a **pie** chart, to make it more meaningful we would like each slice to show the value or percentage of the whole, as shown in the examples earlier in the chapter. To do this we would need to add data labels as follows:

To label a pie chart:

- ■ **right** click on the centre of the pie chart to select all slices, or on one of the slices if it is an exploded pie chart
- ■ select **add data labels**

The values represented by each sector are now displayed.

To change whether we see values or percentages or both:

- ■ **right** click on the centre of the pie chart to select all slices, or on one of the slices if it is an exploded pie chart
- ■ select **format data labels**
- ■ under **Label Options**, check or uncheck **Value** and **Percentage** as required

deleting a chart

Once you have created a chart it is possible that you may wish to delete it and start again, or just remove it from the sheet.

To delete a chart:

- ■ click on the chart to select it
- ■ press **delete**

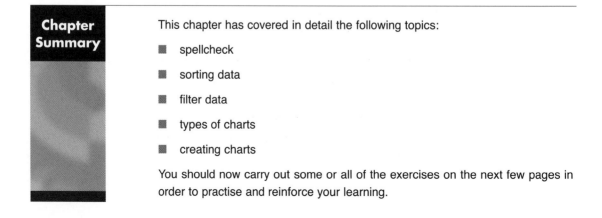

Chapter Summary

This chapter has covered in detail the following topics:

- ■ spellcheck
- ■ sorting data
- ■ filter data
- ■ types of charts
- ■ creating charts

You should now carry out some or all of the exercises on the next few pages in order to practise and reinforce your learning.

Activities

Exercise 1 – using spellcheck and search and replace

In this first exercise we are going to use the built in spellcheck facility and search and replace to make corrections and changes to text within our worksheet. We are again going to make use of an existing spreadsheet which contains data relating to international sales of fashion items.

This spreadsheet contains nearly 40 rows of data relating to sales information: the month of the sale, the category of product, the value, the sales rep that made the sale and the country to which the sale was made. Not all 40 rows will be visible at the same time on the screen images in this book.

The file we are going to use is **Ch7Prodsales**.

Stage 1

This stage uses the built in spellcheck tool within a previously created workbook.

1. Download the workbook Ch7Prodsales.

2. Open the downloaded file, save the workbook with new name **Ch7Exercise1**.

The workbook should appear as shown below:

▲	A	B	C	D	E
1	**Product Sales**				
2					
3	**Month**	**Product**	**Value**	**Sales Rep**	**Country**
4	Jan	Acessories	£125.75	TP	UK
5	Jan	Footwear	£99.95	SM	UK
6	Jan	Lugage	£220.00	PY	GER
7	Feb	Jewelery	£1,500.00	TP	UK
8	Feb	Footwear	£220.00	PY	FR
9	Feb	Jewelery	£67.75	LO	GER
10	Feb	Clothing	£34.90	SM	SP
11	Mar	Footwear	£154.50	PY	GER
12	Mar	Lugage	£124.60	SM	SP
13	Mar	Clothing	£44.75	PY	FR
14	Mar	Acessories	£154.50	LO	SP
15	Apr	Other	£34.90	LO	SP

We are first going to spellcheck a small group of cells.

3.   Select cells B4 to B10 in the Product column.

4.   Select the **Spellcheck** option from the menu.

5.   Step through the individual checks, making corrections as appropriate, choosing the correct spelling from the choices offered.

We can see from the image below, we have already made four corrections to the spellings, in cells B4, B6, B7 and B9:

	A	B	C	D	E	
1	Product Sales					
2						
3	Month	Product	Value	Sales Rep	Country	
4	Jan	Accessories	£125.75	TP	UK	
5	Jan	Footwear	£99.95	SM	UK	
6	Jan	Luggage	£220.00	PY	GER	
7	Feb	Jewellery	£1,500.00	TP	UK	
8	Feb	Footwear	£220.00	PY	FR	
9	Feb	Jewellery	£67.75	LO	GER	
10	Feb	Clothing	£34.90	SM	SP	
11	Mar	Footwear	£154.50	PY	GER	
12	Mar	Lugage	£124.60	SM	SP	
13	Mar	Clothing	£44.75	PY	FR	
14	Mar	Acessories	£154.50	LO	SP	
15	Apr	Other	£34.90	LO	SP	

Now we are going to check a whole column.

6.   Select the whole of column B.

7.   Select the **spellcheck** option from the menu.

8.   Step through the individual checks, choosing the correct spelling from the choices offered, and this time select **Change All**, to correct all occurrences in column B which are spelt incorrectly.

9.   Save the workbook with the name **Ch7Exercise1**.

Your spreadsheet should now look as shown on the next page:

◢	A	B	C	D	E
1	**Product Sales**				
2					
3	**Month**	**Product**	**Value**	**Sales Rep**	**Country**
4	Jan	Accessories	£125.75	TP	UK
5	Jan	Footwear	£99.95	SM	UK
6	Jan	Luggage	£220.00	PY	GER
7	Feb	Jewellery	£1,500.00	TP	UK
8	Feb	Footwear	£220.00	PY	FR
9	Feb	Jewellery	£67.75	LO	GER
10	Feb	Clothing	£34.90	SM	SP
11	Mar	Footwear	£154.50	PY	GER
12	Mar	Luggage	£124.60	SM	SP
13	Mar	Clothing	£44.75	PY	FR
14	Mar	Accessories	£154.50	LO	SP
15	Apr	Other	£34.90	LO	SP

Stage 2

We are going to use the **Sort** facility to group together sales of the same product.

Note: one facility which you may need to make use of, which is common to all packages, is the **Undo** button or option. This will allow you to revert the data back a step at a time, undoing your changes or edits. This is particularly useful when sorting data, since if you sort incorrectly and mix up the data, there is no other easy way to get back to where you were before you started to sort the data.

1.   Continue with the workbook **Ch7Exercise1**.

2.   We are going to sort the data by Product (column B). Select all the data and **Sort** alphabetically A to Z. You will need to select **Custom Sort**, otherwise the selected data is automatically sorted by the leftmost column.

Your spreadsheet should appear like the screen image at the top of the next page.

	A	B	C	D	E
1	**Product Sales**				
2					
3	**Month**	**Product**	**Value**	**Sales Rep**	**Country**
4	Jan	Accessories	£125.75	TP	UK
5	Mar	Accessories	£154.50	LO	SP
6	May	Accessories	£144.50	LO	SP
7	Jul	Accessories	£44.75	LO	GER
8	Sep	Accessories	£1,460.40	PY	FR
9	Sep	Accessories	£34.00	PY	GER
10	Oct	Accessories	£67.75	LO	GER
11	Oct	Accessories	£34.90	PY	GER
12	Nov	Accessories	£56.00	PY	FR
13	Dec	Accessories	£124.60	MP	GER
14	Feb	Clothing	£34.90	SM	SP
15	Mar	Clothing	£44.75	PY	FR

3.   We now want to sort the data by Value (column C) in descending order (largest to smallest).

4.   Save the workbook.

Your spreadsheet should appear as shown in the image below:

	A	B	C	D	E
1	**Product Sales**				
2					
3	**Month**	**Product**	**Value**	**Sales Rep**	**Country**
4	Feb	Jewellery	£1,500.00	TP	UK
5	Aug	Other	£1,500.00	PY	FR
6	Dec	Other	£1,500.00	LO	FR
7	Sep	Accessories	£1,460.40	PY	FR
8	Apr	Footwear	£1,460.40	TP	UK
9	Aug	Other	£1,460.40	PY	FR
10	Jun	Clothing	£1,124.60	TP	UK
11	May	Other	£344.90	LO	SP
12	Feb	Footwear	£220.00	PY	FR
13	Jan	Luggage	£220.00	PY	GER
14	Nov	Luggage	£220.00	LO	SP
15	Mar	Accessories	£154.50	LO	SP

Stage 3

We are now going to use this same data to practise using the **Filter** tool.

1.   Continue with the workbook **Ch7Exercise1**.

2.   Select cell A3.

3.   Select the **Filter** tool to apply a filter.

4.   On the Country column, apply a filter so that you can only see rows where the Country is GER.

The workbook should look as shown below:

◢	A	B	C	D	E
1	**Product Sales**				
2					
3	**Month** ▼	**Product** ▼	**Value** ▼	**Sales R** ▼	**Countr** ▼
13	Jan	Luggage	£220.00	PY	GER
17	Mar	Footwear	£154.50	PY	GER
22	Dec	Accessories	£124.60	MP	GER
29	Oct	Accessories	£67.75	LO	GER
30	Feb	Jewellery	£67.75	LO	GER
32	Dec	Luggage	£56.25	LO	GER
33	Apr	Other	£56.25	LO	GER
34	Jul	Other	£56.25	LO	GER
37	Jul	Accessories	£44.75	LO	GER
40	Oct	Accessories	£34.90	PY	GER
43	Sep	Accessories	£34.00	PY	GER

5.   Apply an additional filter to the rows, using the Product column, so that only the rows for Product = Accessories and Country = GER are to be shown.

The workbook should look as shown below. This completes Exercise 1.

◢	A	B	C	D	E
1	**Product Sales**				
2					
3	**Month** ▼	**Product** ▼	**Value** ▼	**Sales R** ▼	**Countr** ▼
22	Dec	Accessories	£124.60	MP	GER
29	Oct	Accessories	£67.75	LO	GER
37	Jul	Accessories	£44.75	LO	GER
40	Oct	Accessories	£34.90	PY	GER
43	Sep	Accessories	£34.00	PY	GER

Exercise 2 – creating bar and line charts

In this exercise we are going to produce a variety of bar charts, using some sales data.

Stage 1

In this stage we are going to create a simple bar chart from some product sales data.

1. Open a new workbook.
2. Enter the data shown in the table below.

Sales by Product						
	Jan	**Feb**	**Mar**	**Apr**	**May**	**June**
Product A	1000	1500	1430	1490	1750	1510
Product B	960	1210	1500	500	1200	1700
Product C	340	860	900	1000	1050	1100

3. Name your worksheet **Data**.
4. Save the workbook with the name **Ch7Exercise2**.
5. Select the cells A2 through to G5, this includes the column headings, row headings and data for the six months for each product.
6. Insert a vertical **bar (column) chart** to represent this data.
7. Move the chart and position it below the data. Resize it to the same width as the data.
8. Using chart **Layout**, **Chart Title** and **Axis Titles** add titles to the chart layout. The Chart Title should be centred and **Overlay**. For the Vertical Axis title, select type Rotated Title.
9. Change the Chart Title to **Sales January to June**.
10. Change the 'y' axis title to **Months**.
11. Add a title for the 'x' axis, and change it to read **Qty**.
12. Save your spreadsheet.

Your spreadsheet should now appear as shown at the top of the next page.

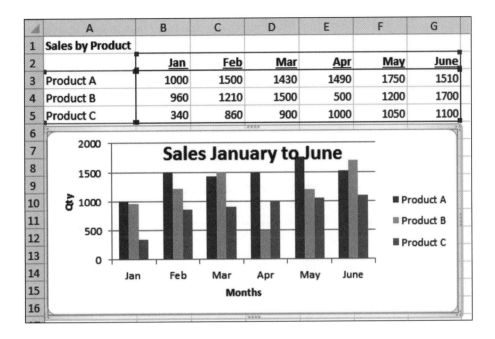

Stage 2

In this stage we are going to manipulate the chart we have created.

1.   **Move** the chart onto a different worksheet – sheet2.

2.   Change the size of the chart so that it covers approximately 13 rows, and 7 columns, starting in cell B2.

3.   Change the **Chart Title** to **Above the Chart** from the Layout menu.

4.   Change the **Chart type** to **Stacked Columns**.

5.   Save your workbook.

Your workbook should look as shown below:

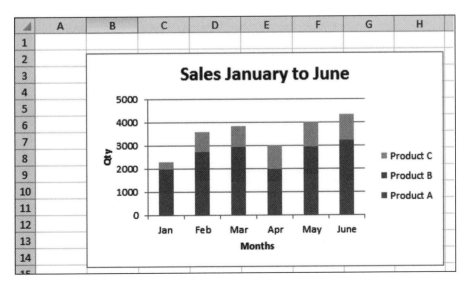

6. Change the graph type to **horizontal bar chart**.

7. You may notice that the alignment of the new 'x' axis label **Qty** is strange. Select the 'x' axis label, and change the alignment to horizontal.

The chart should look as shown below:

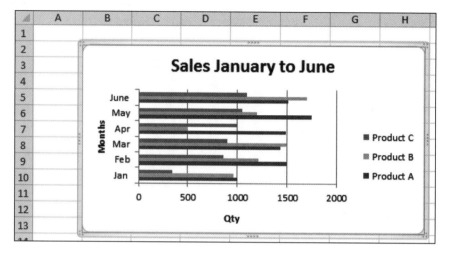

Stage 3

Using the same data we are now going to create a line chart.

1. Select the worksheet **Data**.

We want to produce a line chart just for Product A, so that we can look at the growth (or not) in sales.

2. Select cells A2 through to G3.

3. Insert a chart of type **Line**.

4. Reposition and resize your chart to fit just under the data.

5. Save your workbook.

Your workbook should look as shown below:

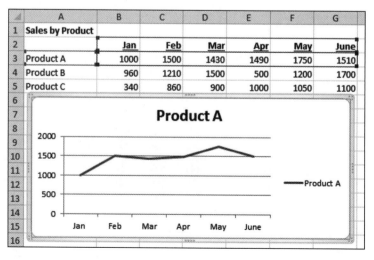

Exercise 3 – creating pie charts

In this exercise we are going to produce pie charts, using some sales data.

Stage 1

In this stage we are going to create a pie chart from some regional sales data.

1. Open a new workbook.

2. Enter the Company sales data for each of the five regions shown in the table below:

Region	Sales
South	210,000
West	155,000
Central	412,000
North	327,000
East	523,000

3. Name your worksheet **Sales**.

4. Save the workbook with the name **Ch7Exercise3**.

5. Create a pie chart to show the sales data by region.

6. Resize and position to the right of the data in your spreadsheet.

Your worksheet should look as shown below:

We are going to add value labels to the slices of the chart.

7.   Add **data labels** to the chart showing the value of sales in each region.

This can be seen in the image below:

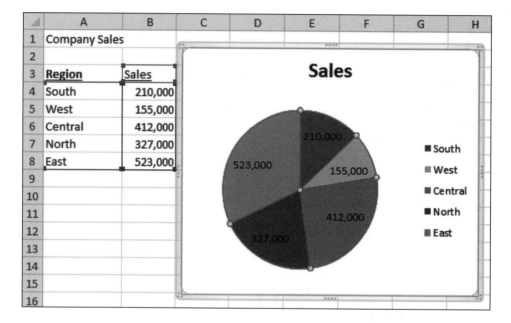

8.   Format the data labels on the chart (using **label options**) to just show **percentages**.

Again this is shown in the image below:

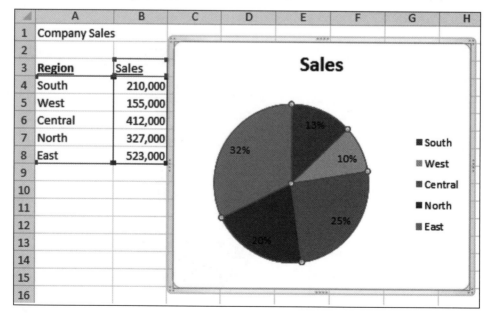

9.   Save your workbook.

Stage 2

In this stage we are going to create an exploded pie chart.

1. Copy the data from the Sales worksheet onto a new worksheet.

2. Name the worksheet Sales – Exploded.

3. Add a further row of sales data for the overseas region.

Region	Sales
Overseas	870,000

4. Create an exploded pie chart for the regional sales data.

5. Move and resize to position to the right of the data.

Your worksheet should look as shown below:

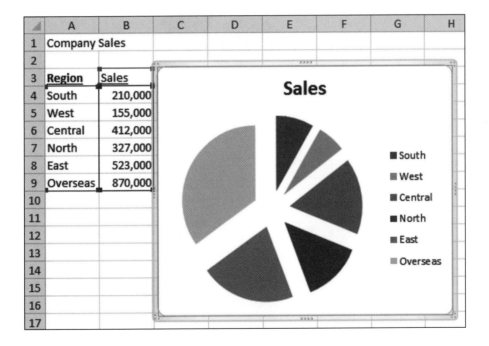

6. Finally we are going to add data labels, and format them to show both the value of sales, and the percentage each slice represents:

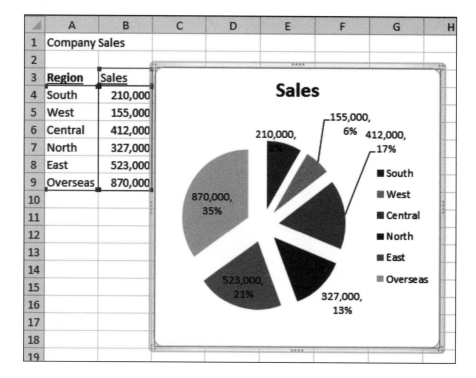

This concludes the exercises for chapter 7.

Index

for your notes

for your notes

for your notes

for your notes

for your notes

_____

for your notes

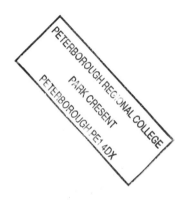